SERIES THE ENCOUNTER SERIES

Jews in Unsecular America

Essays by
Milton Himmelfarb
David Novak
Jonathan D. Sarna
Marvin R. Wilson

Edited by
Richard John Neuhaus

With a Foreword by
Richard John Neuhaus and Ronald B. Sobel

William B. Eerdmans Publishing Company
and
Center for the Study of the American Jewish Experience

Published by Wm. B. Eerdmans Publishing Co.
in cooperation with
The Rockford Institute Center on Religion & Society
and
The Center for the Study of the American Jewish Experience

Library of Congress Cataloging-in-Publication Data

Jews in unsecular America.

(Encounter series ; 6)
Based on a conference cosponsored by Temple Emanu-El and the Rockford
Institute Center on Religion & Society.
Contents: Jewish perceptions of the new assertiveness of religion in
American life / Milton Himmelfarb — Christian America or secular
America? / Jonathan D. Sarna — Changing America or secular
America? / Jonathan D. Sarna— Changing Christian perceptions of Jews in
America / Marvin D. Wilson — [etc.].
    1. Jews — United States — Politics and government — Congresses.
2. Christianity and politics — Congresses.   3. Religion and politics —
United States — Congresses.   4. Judaism — Relations — Christianity —
1945-   — Congresses.   5. Christianity and other religions — Judaism —
1945-   — Congresses.   6. Judaism — United States — Congresses.
7. United States — Ethnic relations — Congresses.
I. Himmelfarb, Milton.   II. Neuhaus, Richard John.
III. Temple Emanu-El (New York, N.Y.)   IV. Center on
Religion & Society (New York, N.Y.)
V. Series: Encounter series (Grand Rapids, Mich.) ; 6.
E184.J5J658   1987   322'.1'089924073   87-24642

ISBN 0-8028-0206-0 (Eerdmans)

Contents

Foreword

The question of how Jews might relate to a predominantly non-Jewish society is hardly new. Indeed, with the exception of the state of Israel, it is a question that Jews face everywhere in the world, and have faced for many centuries. And, of course, the question has a long history also within the American experience. Here and elsewhere that history has been, to put it very gently, a troubled one.

The question may never be settled definitively. The very notion of a definitive settlement belies an understanding of the dynamics, and continuing confusions, of a pluralistic society. But the question and responses to it do take on new forms from time to time, and ours is such a time of new formation. Both Christians and Jews are at the beginning of a quite different discussion of how they should live together as believers and as citizens in America's ongoing experiment in liberal democracy. The way for this discussion has been prepared—perhaps providentially prepared—by the past two decades of interreligious dialogue, which have created a measure of trust between our communities. That trust, which we believe is reflected in the pages that follow, will be sorely needed in the years ahead.

The title "Jews in Unsecular America" indicates the new form of an old question. Contrary to many social theories of the past and present, the evidence is now in that America is far from being a secular society. Measured by all the relevant criteria of belief and behavior, this society seems to be, for better and for worse, incorrigibly and increasingly religious. And, of course, the religion in question is overwhelmingly Christian. In addition, the societal fact of religion is increasingly making itself felt in the public arena. This is a cause for rejoicing among many Christians but a source of puzzlement and anxiety on the part of other Americans, believers and nonbelievers alike. Nowhere is that puzzlement and anxiety more intensely or articulately expressed than among Jewish Americans.

The participants in this conference cosponsored by Temple Emanu-El and the Rockford Institute Center on Religion and Society are Christians and Jews in search of understanding. As the reader will discover, they are determined not to be simply reactive to the new assertiveness of religion in the public square. On the contrary, most of them recognize that this assertiveness contains elements of a healthy democratic impulse to establish stronger connections between public discourse and the ultimate beliefs by which most of us claim to live. But the participants are equally determined not to fudge the hard questions posed by the interaction of religion and politics. Those questions become painfully hard for Jews and others who fear that the "intrusion" of majority religion into our public life may have the result of turning them into strangers in their own land.

The public assertiveness of religion, however, is as much a challenge to Christians as it is to Jews. At least as much. If Jews are not to view a religiously grounded public morality as a threat, it must be unmistakably clear, as it is not now, that Christian morality includes a respect—indeed, a reverence—for the reality of living Judaism. Christians and Jews are together being moved beyond the mistake of thinking that pluralism means public indifference to our unique characteristics as Christians and Jews. Pluralism is not the monism of indifference but the lively engagement of the communal identities, beliefs, and loyalties that make us what we are and who we are.

Such engagement requires that we cultivate the virtues of civility. At a level even more profound and more difficult, it requires that we explore and express the specifically Jewish and Christian warrants for our devotion to a pluralistic and democratic society. This volume helps explain why such an exploration is urgently necessary. It also outlines directions for continuing exploration and expression in the years ahead. Above all, it attempts to show why old questions have assumed new forms both troubling and promising for Jews and Christians in unsecular America.

THE ROCKFORD INSTITUTE   Richard John Neuhaus, Director
Center on Religion & Society
New York City

TEMPLE EMANU-EL   Ronald B. Sobel, Senior Rabbi
New York City

Jewish Perceptions of the New Assertiveness of Religion in American Life

Milton Himmelfarb

1. In 1966 *Commentary* published an article of mine entitled "Church and State: How High a Wall?" It began, "The Jews are probably more devoted than anyone else in America to the separation of church and state." That is probably still so. The 1984 National Survey of American Jews, conducted for the American Jewish Committee by Steven M. Cohen, showed American Jews to be ambivalent about some things but not about separation.

Thus, in answer to one question in the questionnaire, three in four agreed that they supported "such government programs as welfare and food stamps," while in answer to the very next question two in three agreed that "such government programs as welfare and food stamps have had many bad effects on the very people they're supposed to help." The successiveness of the questions should have discouraged contradiction and ambivalence. Apparently it did not.

Contrariwise, placing similar questions far apart could be expected to encourage forgetfulness, and therefore contradiction and ambivalence. With church-state issues that did not work.

Most Americans favor tuition tax credits for parents of children in private or parochial schools. Question 3 asked about that, and question 41 about tuition tax credits for parents of children in Jewish day schools. The answers to both questions were essentially identical: of those having an opinion, two to one opposed tuition tax credits, and only one in eleven or twelve was unsure. Opposition to "a moment of silent meditation each day in the public schools" was even stronger: more than three to one, with one in eleven not sure.

1

In 1985 Cohen sent questionnaires to the same people who had answered the 1984 National Survey of American Jews and got more than five hundred returns. One question was designed to test whether the attitudes of American Jews toward abortion are the same in the United States and Israel. It turns out that they are much the same. About four in five said they opposed both American and Israeli governmental prohibition of abortion except in the case of rape, incest, or danger to the mother's life; one in eight favored the prohibition, and one in ten or twelve was unsure.

On the other hand, there is a clear difference in response to "teaching about religion in the public schools." Jews oppose such teaching in the United States more than three to one, while more (though fewer than half) favor than oppose it in Israel.

	Yes	No	Not Sure
U.S.	20%	70%	10%
Israel	47	38	15

This last may be less inconsistent than it looks. Someone who is against teaching about religion in American public schools but for it in Israeli public schools might try to justify himself in some such way as this: In America children study English literature; in Israel they study Hebrew literature. Though the King James version is an English literary classic, you can teach English literature without the Bible. You cannot very well teach Hebrew literature without the Bible.

Note, however, that only about one in four said yes to teaching about religion in Israeli public schools and no to teaching about religion in American schools. Further, that fully three in eight American Jews oppose teaching about religion even in Israeli public schools shows a certain universalization of American values and practice.

2. From an American perspective it is anomalous that most American Jews vote conspicuously to the left of their bankbooks, because other American religious and ethnic groups do not. From a worldwide Jewish perspective it is not at all anomalous, because at least until recently that is how most Jews in Western countries have voted.

What is the right perspective for viewing the strong separationism of most American Jews? If the alternative to separationism is Throne-and-Altarism, then modern Jews everywhere are all separationists. Yet British Jews, and of late even some French Jews, find it hard to understand why American Jews are so intense in their dislike for such things as silent meditation and teaching about religion in the public schools. American Jews might answer that they have higher expectations of the United States than British Jews have of Great Britain or French Jews of France. In the 1984 survey, five of six Jews agreed that "the U.S. has offered Jews more opportunities and freedom than any other diaspora country." (One in sixteen disagreed, and one in ten was not sure.)

How are we to understand the dominant attitude of American Jews toward, say, the Moral Majority?

1984 Impression of	Generally Favorable	Generally Unfavorable	Mixed	No Impression
ACLU	42%	13%	24%	22%
NAACP	54	12	28	6
Moral Majority	7	69	14	10

Maybe our respondents answered in this way because they are Jews, maybe because on the whole they are educated Americans, and maybe because they are both. In 1984 only one in six had never been to college, three in five had graduated, and more had at least one graduate degree than had a baccalaureate alone. About the Moral Majority, at any rate, the unpopularity-to-popularity ratio of ten to one would probably not be greatly different in any respectable faculty club. Which is to say that to Jews "Jerry Falwell"—the type, not the actual man—may look like Elmer Gantry as well as Torquemada.

In 1985 Cohen tempted his respondents to do as some neoconservative intellectuals do—to think better of the Christian Right on account of Israel: "Since the Christian Right has been very pro-Israel, American Jews should overlook their objections to the Christian Right's ideas about America and work more closely with it to help Israel." Though the wording took for granted Jewish "objections to the Christian's Right's ideas about America," few were mollified. Only a fifth agreed; more than half disagreed, and more than a quarter were unsure. Particularist considerations—"help Israel"—are not allowed to prevail over loyalty to liberal "ideas about America," whether political or cultural. This loyalty, in turn, is itself not without a certain admixture of Jewish particularism. Liberalism has long been held to be not only good in itself but also "good for the Jews."

3. People use denial or evasion for dealing with conflict between one good and another. Dovishness is a liberal good. The 1985 questionnaire asked for agreement or disagreement with the proposition that "major reductions in U.S. defense spending . . . will weaken the security of the U.S." A clear majority disagreed—that is, those disagreeing exceeded the sum of those agreeing and those not sure. The contradictory desires for major reductions in defense spending and for national security are reconciled by denying that they are contradictory.

Denial or evasion is also at work in American Jews' assessment of the effects of religion on society. Asked in 1984 whether they agreed or disagreed with the proposition that "the decline of religion in American life has contributed to a decline in morality," the six in seven who had an opinion divided about equally. It may be that some of those who said they disagreed actually did agree but did not want to say so for fear of giving aid and comfort to the Moral Majority. But the reasoning, if that is the right name for it, could also have gone the other way: the Moral Majority is wrong; the Moral Majority says that the decline of religion in American life has contributed to a decline in morality; therefore the decline of religion in American life has not contributed to a decline in morality.

That is denial. Evasion could take this form: Decline of religion? What decline? The Christian Right and those scary pro-lifers are evidence of a rise rather than a decline of religion. Decline in morality? If by morality you mean chastity, you are probably right, but morality is more than that. It also includes such things as tolerance and lack of prejudice. Since America is more tolerant and less prejudiced now than only a generation ago, you could as easily report a rise as a decline of morality. Besides, it is not as if we were against chastity. In the same survey three in four agreed that "adultery is wrong"; one in six disagreed, and one in ten was not sure. (This recalls the old rabbinical—or is it generically clerical?—joke about the letter that the hospitalized rabbi receives from the secretary of the congregation: "Dear Rabbi, The trustees have instructed me to send you their best wishes for a speedy recovery, by a vote of five to four.")

4. After we dispose of the denial and evasion, we are still left with something serious that needs to be explained. The question about the decline of religion and morality is central. Put another way, it might be this: Is religion a Good Thing or a Bad Thing for society? Not every religionist will say that it is necessarily a good thing. Though peace is presumably good and the sword bad, the scriptures of a great religion promise not peace but a sword. Nor will every secularist say that religion is a bad thing. For personally irreligious people such as Emile Durkheim and Max Weber, the very asking about the goodness or badness of religion for society might well have seemed as foolish as asking about the goodness or badness of breathing: No life without breathing, no social life without religion. The very *philosophes* whose battle cry was *écrasez l'infâme* and who privately scoffed at the idea that their deistic deity had considerately provided an afterlife to mortal men and women were also convinced that in order for society to endure, the masses must not be disabused of their belief in an afterlife of rewards and punishments.

5. Why then the even split between Jews agreeing and disagreeing about religious and moral decline in the United States? Let us imagine a Jew who is apprehensive about the new assertiveness of religion in American life. What might such a person say?

He might start by saying that he was typical rather than untypical in being apprehensive—about the new assertiveness of religion, of course, but also about nearly everything else. A kind of free-floating anxiety is the American Jewish norm. The same people who in 1984 said that Jews as a minority fared better in the United States than anywhere else also, and at the same time, *denied*, by almost five to four, with one in seven or eight not sure, that "antisemitism in America is currently"—currently, not in some all-too-possible future—"not a serious problem for American Jews." At a time when Jews have been more successful than ever before, above all in politics, they deny by almost two to one, with one in nine not sure, that "virtually all positions of influence in America are open to Jews." From the outside, American Jews must resemble the poor little rich girl.

The apprehensiveness of us Jews is not altogether without locus or focus. Mostly we see unfriendliness if not downright hostility more among the rich and powerful than among the poor and powerless. (We make an exception for blacks. In 1984 a little more than half of us thought most or many blacks anti-Semitic.) About Republicans 29 percent of us thought most or many to be anti-Semitic, about Democrats only 6 percent; about conservatives 35 percent, about liberals 7 percent. Averaging those anti-Semitism ratings, we arrive at something like a 15 or 20 percent anti-Semitism rating by Jews for all Americans (all white Americans?) *in their secular capacity*. In their religious, Christian capacity we think them more anti-Semitic than that. In 1984, 40 percent of us thought most or many Catholics anti-Semitic, 42 percent of mainstream Protestants, and 46 percent of fundamentalist Protestants. In 1985 one of the questions asked about American Christians, American Jews, and Israelis was whether each of these groups was "basically like me." Naturally, American Jews got the highest vote, more than three quarters. Next came Israelis, with something less than half. Only a little more than a third considered American Christians to be "basically like me."

6. And what is this talk about the new assertiveness of religion? (The representative Jew is still talking.) People speak not language in general but a language in particular, and they profess not religion in general but a religion in particular. It is not a new assertiveness of religion that makes Jews uneasy, it is the new assertiveness of Christianity, or of some movements and tendencies in Christianity. Nor is the assertiveness new. It is simply renewed. Some of us experienced it when we were young.

Warner and Srole's *Social Systems of American Ethnic Groups*, published in 1945, is about a New England city ten years earlier. In the public schools the Lord's Prayer was recited every morning. When the authors asked a Jewish boy what he did about it, he answered that he recited it too, "because when in Rome do as the Romans do." When in America do as the Americans do. Americans recite the Lord's Prayer. Since it is a Christian prayer, the real Americans must be Christian.

Since it is not my prayer, I, the Jewish schoolboy, must be something other or less than a real American.

Morris B. Abram, more conservative now than he used to be, still writes about how "very uncomfortable" he was "as a child in South Georgia public school system—really a Protestant operation supported by public funds—when the time came to recite the hymns and mumble the prayers." At the end of August 1985 a letter to the editor of the Washington *Post* protested the linkage, or hyphen, in Secretary of Education William Bennett's reference to America's "Judeo-Christian" heritage:

> It is almost as though the users of the phrase believe . . . that Jews should not be critical of the users' religious agenda as long as that agenda begins with the prefix "Judeo." . . . I grew up as a member of one of three Jewish families in a town of 1,600 in northern New Jersey. Each day in public school we read from the Bible, said the Lord's Prayer and sang "Jesus Loves Me." . . . To most of us, school prayer means the prayers of other people's faiths . . . and reemphasis of our status as a "minority" religion.

To young American Jews in the bad old days the assertiveness of religion in American life meant conformity, keeping a low profile, not making waves—prudence at the expense of self-respect. It fostered Jewish self-hate, the internalization of the Other's image of Jews as alien and inferior.

Young Jews today have it better than their grandparents had when young, and one reason may be that the Lord's Prayer is no longer recited in public schools. We are not nostalgic about those days, and we doubt that some of the new asserters of religion in American life are equally lacking in nostalgia.

In 1985 Senator Boschwitz of Minnesota sent to a Jewish list a fund-raising letter on behalf of the 1986 reelection campaign of Senator Specter of Pennsylvania. (Both are Republicans and both are Jews.) Boschwitz's letter stressed Specter's part in the legislative fight against mandating or allowing prayer in the public schools and urged his reelection for guarding the wall of separation against those who would breach it. The result in money raised was phenomenal, perhaps a record.

7. A penultimate word about Orthodox Jews. Qualitatively of great and growing importance in the American Jewish community, quantitatively they are a small minority, fewer than ten percent. On the one hand, they generally are no less suspicious than other Jews of Christian intentions, though from a different angle—interreligious dialogue, for example. On the other hand, they are less separationist, if only from self-interest. Probably a majority—certainly a plurality—of the parents of

children in Jewish day schools are Orthodox and resent the opposition of most other Jews to tuition tax credits.

8. My own views have changed little in the almost twenty years since that *Commentary* article of mine. I have quoted its first sentence. Its last sentence was Robert Frost's "Something there is that doesn't love a wall."

To the position that has been dominant in the American Jewish community for the past forty years or so Naomi Cohen, in her *Encounter with Emancipation: The German Jews in the United States 1830–1940*, contrasts an earlier position:

> Jews usually meant a neutral-to-all religions rather than a divorced-from-religion state. Indeed, the later concept . . . was as abhorrent to Jews as it was to most Americans. Rabbis, long the most influential leaders of the community, taught that religion was a vital component of the good life and, like Christian clergymen, inveighed against the inroads of secularization. Louis Marshall, the national spokesman of American Jews on the eve of World War I, found nothing intrinsically offensive about Bible reading in the public schools, so long as it did not become sectarian.

New is not necessarily improved.

Christian America or Secular America? The Church-State Dilemma of American Jews

Jonathan D. Sarna

"The government of the United States of America is not in any sense founded on the Christian religion." This statement, found in Article 11 of a 1797 treaty between the United States and the Bey and subjects of Tripoli, encapsulates what may safely be seen as a near-unanimous Jewish view on the relationship of church and state in America. It is a manifestly negative view, a statement of what America is not. It also turns out to be somewhat of a fraud, since the article in question does not appear in the Arabic original of this treaty—a fact discovered only some 133 years later. It is, however, a classic text, "cited hundreds of times in numerous court cases and in political debates whenever the issue of church-state relations arose"[1] to reassure the faithful that *no* religion obtains special treatment in America. Christianity might be the law of the land in other countries; here, American Jews have insisted, religious liberty is guaranteed by the Constitution itself.

But what does religious liberty mean? How are those who adhere to the religion of the majority, those who adhere to the religion of the minority, and those who adhere to no religion at all supposed to inter-relate? And if America is not a Christian society, what kind of society is it

---

1. Morton Borden, *Jews, Turks, and Infidels* (Chapel Hill, N.C.: University of North Carolina Press, 1984), pp. 76-79.

8

and what is the relationship of that society to the state? American Jews, especially since they have insisted that the "Christian America" model is wrong, have an obligation to respond to these questions and to propose alternative models of what the relationship of church and state in America should be. How well they have fulfilled this obligation remains unclear, since no full-scale account of American Jewish thinking on these matters has yet appeared, and most of the literature that does exist is unfortunately more polemical than scholarly. Yet even the superficial survey I have undertaken here is sufficient to warrant the following conclusions: (1) American Jews *have* put forward alternative models, (2) their views on church and state have been more diverse than generally imagined, and (3) in struggling with these issues they have confronted two basic challenges: (a) the challenge to participate as equals in majority society without embracing the majority's religion and (b) the challenge to decide whether Jewish interests are better served under a system that guarantees equality to *all* religions or one that mandates complete state separation from *any* religion.

1

The idea that America is a Christian nation has its roots in the colonial period and continues as an unbroken tradition down to the present day. "From the beginning," Robert T. Handy explains, "American Protestants entertained a lively hope that some day the civilization of the country would be fully Christian. The ways in which the hope was expressed and the activities it engendered varied somewhat from generation to generation, but for more than three centuries Protestants drew direction and inspiration from the vision of a Christian America. It provided a common orientation that cut across denominational differences, and furnished goals toward which all could work, each in his own style and manner."[2] The Constitution and Bill of Rights (which, of course, applied only at the federal level and did not become binding upon the states until the twentieth century) did not dampen the ardor of those who embraced the Christian America ideal, for they interpreted these documents narrowly. Their reading—and whether it was a correct one or not is less important than the fact that they believed it to be true— was summed up by Justice Joseph Story in his famous *Commentaries on the Constitution* (1833):

> The real object of the amendment was, not to countenance, much less to advance Mahometanism, or Judaism, or infidelity, by pros-

---

2. Handy, A *Christian America* (New York: Oxford University Press, 1971), p. viii.

trating Christianity; but to exclude all rivalry among Christian
sects, and to prevent any ecclesiastical establishment, which
should give to an hierarchy the exclusive patronage of the national
government.[3]

Story's view was buttressed by various notable court decisions
which, in accordance with British precedent, assumed that "the Christian religion is recognized as constituting a part of the common law."[4]
Chancellor James Kent, chief justice of New York's highest court, held
in 1811 that religious freedom and church-state separation did not stand
in the way of a common law indictment for malicious blasphemy, for
"We are a Christian people and the morality of the country is deeply
ingrafted upon Christianity." One hundred twenty years later, in 1931,
the same phrase—"we are a Christian people"—was used by the United
States Supreme Court in a decision known as *U.S. v. Macintosh*. In
1939, the Georgia Supreme Court, in upholding a Sunday closing law,
forthrightly declared America to be "a Christian nation."[5]

Individual Americans have been even more outspoken in associat-
ing the state with the religion of the majority. Daniel Webster, for
example, argued eloquently before the Supreme Court in the case of
Vidal v. Girard's Executors (1844) that "the preservation of Christianity
is one of the main ends of government," that a school "derogatory to the
Christian religion" or even a school "for the teaching of the Jewish
religion" should "not be regarded as a charity," an' that "All, all, proclaim that Christianity . . . is the law of the land." He lost his case but
won cheers from members of the Whig Party. Furthermore, his views
with regard to the illegitimacy of schools "for the propagation of Judaism" won support from the Court even as it rejected his claims on other

----

3. Story, *Commentaries on the Constitution of the United States* (Boston:
Hillard, Gray, 1833), III, par. 1865, as quoted in Chester J. Antieau et al.,
Freedom from Federal Establishment (Milwaukee: Bruce Publishing, 1964),
p. 160; cf. Michael J. Malbin, *Religion and Politics: The Intentions of the
Authors of the First Amendment* (Washington: American Enterprise Institute for
Public Policy Research, 1978).
4. *Shover v. The State*, 5 Eng. 259, as quoted by Bernard J. Meislin in
"Jewish Law in America," in *Jewish Law in Legal History and the Modern
World*, ed. Bernard S. Jackson (Leiden: E. J. Brill, 1980), p. 159; cf. Borden,
Jews, Turks, and Infidels, pp. 97-129.
5. *People v. Ruggles*, 8 Johns Rep. (N.Y.) 294 (1811); *U.S. v. Macintosh*
283 U.S. 605 (1931); *Rogers v. State*, 60 Ga. App. 722; cf. John Webb Pratt,
Religion, Politics and Diversity (Ithaca, N.Y.: Cornell University Press, 1967),
pp. 138, 142; Leonard W. Levy, *Treason against God: A History of the Offense
of Blasphemy* (New York: Schocken Books, 1981), p. 334; and Meislin, "Jewish
Law in America," p. 159.

grounds.[6] Webster may well have changed his mind later on.[7] Still, the views he expressed in this case clearly reflected the sentiments of a significant minority of Americans, in his day and many decades afterward as well.

2

American Jews have, broadly speaking, offered two meaningful alternatives to the claims of "Christian America." Both of them are historically well grounded, both appeal to American Constitutional ideals, and both claim to promote American and Jewish interests. One stresses the broadly religious (as distinct from narrowly Christian) character of the American people; the other stresses church-state separation and the attendant secular nature of the American government. They reflect different readings of history, involve Jews with different kinds of friends and allies, and translate into radically different policy positions.

The first response conjures up an image of Americans as a religious people, committed to no religion in particular but certain that some kind of religion is necessary for the well-being of all citizens. This idea finds its most important early legislative expression in the Northwest Ordinance of 1787, in which "religion, morality and knowledge"—not further defined—are termed "necessary to good government and the happiness of mankind." Leading Americans from Benjamin Franklin (who proposed that nondenominational prayers be recited at the Constitutional Convention) to Dwight D. Eisenhower ("Our form of government has no sense unless it is founded in a deeply felt religious faith, and I don't care what it is") have championed similar views, as have some proponents of what is now known as civil religion.[8] The concept is somewhat nebulous,

6. *The Works of Daniel Webster* (Boston: Little, Brown, 1851), 6: 175, 166, 176; cf. Anson P. Stokes and Leo Pfeffer, *Church and State in the United States*, rev. ed. (New York: Harper & Row, 1964), p. 105; and Borden, *Jews, Turks and Infidels*, pp. 102-3.

7. See Ferenc M. Szasz, "Daniel Webster—Architect of America's 'Civil Religion,'" *Historical New Hampshire* 34 (1979): 223-43; and Max J. Kohler, "Daniel Webster and the Jews," *Publications of the American Jewish Historical Society* 11 (1903): 186-87.

8. See Benjamin Franklin "Motion for Prayers in the Philadelphia Convention," in *A Benjamin Franklin Reader*, ed. N. G. Goodman (New York: Thomas Y. Crowell, 1945), p. 242; and Patrick Henry, "'And I Don't Care What It Is': The Tradition-History of a Civil Religion Proof-Text," *The Journal of the American Academy of Religion* 49 (1981): 41. Cf. *American Civil Religion*, ed. Russell E. Richey and Donald G. Jones (New York: Harper & Row, 1974); John F. Wilson, *Public Religion in American Culture* (Philadelphia: Temple University Press, 1979); and Martin E. Marty, "A Sort of Republican Banquet," *The Journal of Religion* 59 (October 1979): 383-405.

and means different things to different people. What is important here, however, is the existence of an ongoing tradition, dating back to the early days of the republic, that links Americans to religion without entering into any particulars. It is a tradition that counts Judaism in among all other American faiths, Christian and non-Christian alike.

This tradition, although rarely appealed to by American Jews today, forms the basis for almost every important American Jewish call for religious freedom in the early decades following independence. A 1783 Jewish petition to the Council of Censors in Pennsylvania, for example, attacked a test oath demanding belief in the divinity "of the old and new Testament" on the grounds that it conflicted with the state's own declaration of rights—"that no man *who acknowledges the being of a God* can be justly deprived or abridged of any civil rights as citizen, on account of his religious sentiments." That this declaration of rights, while inclusive of Jews, allied the state with theism did not trouble Jews at all; indeed, Jonas Phillips, in another petition on the same subject, declared that "the Israelites will think themself [*sic*] happy to live under a government where all Religious societies are on an Equal footing." Jews, in short, sought religious equality, not a state divorced from religion altogether. When efforts were made in 1809 to deny Jacob Henry of North Carolina his seat for refusing to subscribe to a Christian test oath, he underscored this point: "If a man fulfills the duties of *that religion which his education or his Conscience has pointed to him as the true one*; no person, I hold, in this our land of liberty has a right to arraign him at the bar of any inquisition."[9]

Nowhere in any of these statements do Jews suggest that their rights should stand on an equal basis with those of nonbelievers. Nor did Jews protest when several states, including Pennsylvania and Maryland (in the famous "Jew Bill" of 1826), accorded them rights that nonbelievers were denied. Instead, most early American Jews accepted religious freedom as a right rooted within a religious context; they defined it, in the words of Mordecai Noah, perhaps the leading Jewish figure of the day, as "a mere abolition of all religious disabilities." Jews did not mind that America firmly committed itself to religion; their concern was mainly to ensure that this commitment carried with it a guarantee to them that, as Noah put it, "You are free to worship God in any manner you please; and this liberty of conscience cannot be violated."[10]

---

9. These documents are conveniently reprinted in Morris U. Schappes's *Documentary History of the Jews in the United States, 1654-1875*, 3d ed. (New York: Schocken Books, 1971), pp. 64, 68, 122 (italics mine).

10. Schappes, A *Documentary History of the Jews*, p. 279; cf. Jonathan D. Sarna, *Jacksonian Jew: The Two Worlds of Mordecai Noah* (New York: Holmes & Meier, 1981), pp. 132-35.

Jewish support for this essentially proreligion position remained strong throughout the first two thirds of the nineteenth century. One well-versed student of the subject, Shlomith Yahalom, concludes in her recent doctoral dissertation that American Jews during this period were concerned with "freedom *of* religion and not freedom *from* religion." Rather than siding with the demands of antireligious organizations, she writes, many Jews supported "impartial aid to *all* religions."[11] A prime example of this is the fact that during the Civil War, advocates of "Christian America" limited the appointment of chaplains to those who were termed "regularly ordained minister[s] of some Christian denomination." When a Jewish chaplain was refused on this basis, Jews naturally responded with vigorous protests. What they sought, however, was not an abolition of the chaplaincy, as a secularist interpretation of America's religious tradition might have demanded, but only religious equality. When the law was changed so that the word "Christian" was construed to mean "religious," allowing chaplains of the Jewish faith to be appointed, the Jewish community pronounced itself satisfied.[12] Nor was this a unique case. As professor Naomi Cohen explains in her recent book on German Jews in the United States,

> The Jewish pioneers for religious equality generally asked for government neutrality on matters of religion . . . a neutral-to-all-religions rather than a divorced-from-religion state. Indeed, the latter concept, which in the climate of the nineteenth century was tantamount to an anti-religion stance, was as abhorrent to Jews as it was to most Americans. Rabbis, long the most influential leaders of the community, taught that religion was a vital component of the good life and, like Christian clergymen, inveighed against the inroads of secularization.[13]

While this response to the challenge of "Christian America" never completely lost its appeal, Jews in the last third of the nineteenth century found to their dismay that calls for religious equality fell more and more on deaf ears. The spiritual crisis and internal divisions that plagued Protestant America during this period—a period that confronted all American religious groups with the staggering implications of Dar-

---

11. Yahalom, "American Judaism and the Question of Separation between Church and State," Ph.D. diss., Hebrew University, 1981, English section, p. 14; cf. Hebrew section, p. 260.
12. See Bertram W. Korn, *American Jewry and the Civil War* (New York: Atheneum, 1970), pp. 56-97.
13. Cohen, *Encounter with Emancipation: The German Jews in the United States, 1830-1914* (Philadelphia: Jewish Publication Society of America, 1984), p. 77.

winism and biblical criticism—drove evangelicals and liberals alike to
renew their particularistic calls for a "Christian America." Evangelical
leaders championed antimodernist legislation to protect the "Christian
Sabbath," to institute "Christian temperance," to reintroduce Christianity into the schoolroom, and to write Christian morality into American law codes.[14] Liberal Christians may have been somewhat more
circumspect, but, as Robert Handy indicates, their goal too was "in many
respects a spiritualized and idealized restatement of the search for a
specifically Christian society in an age of freedom and progress."[15] The
implication, spelled out by one writer in the *American Presbyterian and
Theological Review*, was that non-Protestants could *never* win full acceptance as equals:

> This is a Christian Republic, our Christianity being of the Protes-
> tant type. People who are not Christians, and people called Chris-
> tians, but who are not Protestants dwell among us, but they did not
> build this house. We have never shut our doors against them, but if
> they come, they must take up with such accommodations as we
> have. . . . If any one, coming among us finds that this arrange-
> ment is uncomfortable, perhaps he will do well to try some other
> country. The world is wide; there is more land to be possessed; let
> him go and make a beginning for himself as our fathers did for us; as
> for this land, we have taken possession of it in the name of the Lord
> Jesus Christ; and if he will give us grace to do it, we mean to hold it
> for him till he comes.[16]

A proposed "Christian Amendment" designed to write "the Lord Jesus
Christ" and the "Christian" basis of national life into the text of the
Constitution attempted to ensure that these aims would be speedily
realized.[17]

Jews, new to America and all-too-familiar with the anti-Jewish
rhetoric of Christian romantics in Europe, were understandably alarmed
by these efforts. As in the old world, so in the new, they thought,

---

14. See Ferenc M. Szasz, "Protestantism and the Search for Stability:
Liberal and Conservative Quests for a Christian America, 1875-1925," in
Building the Organizational Society, ed. Jerry Israel (New York: Free Press,
1972), pp. 88-102; Paul A. Carter, *The Spiritual Crisis of the Gilded Age*
(De Kalb, Ill.: Northern Illinois University Press, 1971); and Jackson Lears, *No
Place of Grace: Antimodernism and the Transformation of American Culture,
1880-1920* (New York: Pantheon Books, 1981).
15. Handy, *A Christian America*, p. 101.
16. *American Protestant Theological Review* 5 (July 1867): 390-91.
17. See Borden, *Jews, Turks, and Infidels*, pp. 62-74; and Cohen, *Encounter with Emancipation*, pp. 254-56.

proponents of religion were allying themselves with the forces of reaction. In search of a safe haven, many Jews now settled firmly down in the freethinking liberal camp; it seemed far more hospitable to Jewish interests. Jews also turned increasingly toward a more radical response to "Christian America"—the doctrine of strict separation.

3

Church-state separation is, of course, an old idea in America; its roots lie deeply imbedded in colonial and European thought. The idea in its most radical form was embraced by Thomas Jefferson, who believed, at least for much of his life, that the state should be utterly secular, religion being purely a matter of personal preference. "The legitimate powers of government," Jefferson wrote in his *Notes on Virginia*, "extend to such acts only as are injurious to others. But it does me no injury for my neighbor to say there are twenty gods or no God." Jefferson refused to proclaim so much as a Thanksgiving Day, lest he "indirectly assume to the United States an authority over religious exercises." We owe to him the famous interpretation of the First Amendment as "a wall of separation between church and state."[18]

It is by no means clear when Jews first began to express support for this model of "secular government." In the election of 1800, a majority of the few thousand Jews in the country supported Jefferson, but not on the basis of his religious views. Indeed, Benjamin Nones, a Philadelphia Jewish merchant and broker, pointed out in Jefferson's defense that the future president "in his very introduction to the Declaration of Independence, declared all men equal, and implores a Divine Providence"—a clear indication of where Nones's own priorities lay.[19] Isaac Leeser, the most important Jewish religious leader of the pre–Civil War period, stood much closer to the radical Jeffersonian view. He repeatedly invoked the principle of church-state separation in defense of Jewish rights, took an active role in the battle for Jewish equality on the state level, and was vigilant in his opposition to such alleged Christian intrusions into American public life as Sunday closing laws, Christian pronouncements in Thanksgiving proclamations, official references to Christianity in state and federal laws, and Christian prayers and Bible readings in public

---

18. Jefferson, quoted by Stokes in *Church and State in the United States*, pp. 52-53; cf. *American State Papers Bearing on Sunday Legislation*, ed. W. A. Blakely (New York: National Religious Liberty Association, 1891), p. 57).

19. See Edwin Wolf II and Maxwell Whiteman, *The History of the Jews of Philadelphia from Colonial Times to the Age of Jackson* (Philadelphia: Jewish Publication Society of America, 1975), p. 213.

schools. Even Leeser, however, was primarily motivated by a desire to assure Jews equal rights and to prevent their assimilation into the mainstream. While he was more wary of religious intrusions into public life than were some of his Jewish contemporaries, he did not literally advocate a secular government, much less an atheistic one.[20]

It was, then, only in the post–Civil War era, with the revival of efforts to create a "Christian America" and the resulting ties between Jews and advocates of religious radicalism and free thought (themselves on the rise during this period), that American Jews began unequivocally to speak out for a government free of any religious influence. Leading Jews participated in such groups as the Free Religious Association and the National Liberal League, and many Jews, among them such notable Reform Jewish leaders as Rabbis Isaac Mayer Wise, Bernhard Felsenthal, and Max Schlesinger, as well as the Jewish lay leader Moritz Ellinger, came to embrace the separationist agenda spelled out in such periodicals as *The Index*, edited by Francis Abbot. As Professor Benny Kraut has pointed out, during this period "the issue of church-state relations precipitated a natural, pragmatic alliance uniting Jews, liberal Christians, religious freethinkers, and secularists in common bond, their religious and theological differences notwithstanding."[21] The result, particularly in terms of Reform Jewish thought, was a clear shift away from emphasis on Americans as a religious people and toward greater stress on government as a secular institution. In 1869 Isaac Mayer Wise proclaimed that "the State has no religion. Having no religion, it cannot impose any religious instruction on the citizen, adult or child."[22] Bernhard Felsenthal, in an 1875 polemic written to prove that "ours is not a Christian civilization," went even further:

> God be praised that church and state are separated in our country! God be praised that the constitutions of the United States and of the single states are now all freed from this danger-breeding idea! God be praised that they are "atheistical," as they have been accused of being by some over-zealous, dark warriors who desire to overcome

20. See Maxie S. Seller, "Isaac Leeser, Architect of the American Jewish Community," Ph.D. diss., University of Pennsylvania, 1965, pp. 136-75; cf. Isaac Leeser, *The Claims of the Jews to an Equality of Rights* (Philadelphia: C. Sherman, 1841).

21. Kraut, "Frances E. Abbot: Perceptions of a Nineteenth Century Religious Radical on Jews and Judaism," in *Studies in the American Jewish Experience*, ed. J. R. Marcus and A. J. Peck (Cincinnati: American Jewish Archives, 1981), pp. 99-101.

22. Wise, quoted by James Heller in *Isaac M. Wise: His Life, Work and Thought* (New York: Union of American Hebrew Congregations, 1965), p. 620.

the nineteenth century and to restore again the fourteenth century. God be praised that this has been accomplished in our Union and may our constitutions and state institutions remain "atheistical" just as our manufactories, our banks, and our commerce are.[23]

This soon became the standard Jewish line on church and state. The Union of American Hebrew Congregations, founded in 1873 (and not originally an organ of the Reform movement), devoted one of its first resolutions to an expression of support for the "Congress of Liberals" in its efforts "to secularize the State completely."[24] The Central Conference of American Rabbis, the American Jewish Committee, and the American Jewish Congress expressed similar support for "strict separationism" early in the twentieth century.[25] A recent study indicates that no significant deviation from this position was yet in evidence even as late as the early 1960s:

> American Jews under the leadership of their defense organizations went on record time after time in significant court cases on behalf of separation. . . . For the most part they eschewed completely the idea of equal government recognition of all religions or of non-denominational religious practices, and they called for non-recognition of *any* form of religion.[26]

More recently, however, the coalition between Jews and secularists has come under increasing pressure. Beginning in the 1960s, Orthodox Jews abandoned their opposition to state aid to parochial schools in the hope of obtaining funds for their own day schools. They argued, as

---

23. Felsenthal, in W. Gunther Plaut's *The Growth of Reform Judaism* (New York: World Union for Progressive Judaism, 1965), pp. 180-81.

24. The full text of this July 1876 resolution is reprinted in *Where We Stand: Social Action Resolutions Adopted by the Union of American Hebrew Congregations* (New York: Union of American Hebrew Congregations, 1960), p. 14.

25. See Eugene Lipman, "The Conference Considers Relations between Religion and the State," in *Retrospect and Prospect*, ed. B. W. Korn (New York: Central Conference of American Rabbis, 1965), pp. 114-28; Naomi W. Cohen, *Not Free to Desist: A History of the American Jewish Committee* (Philadelphia: Jewish Publication Society of America, 1972), 433-52; and Leo Pfeffer, "An Autobiographical Sketch," in *Religion and the State: Essays in Honor of Leo Pfeffer*, ed. James E. Wood, Jr. (Waco, Tex.: Baylor University Press, 1985), pp. 487-533.

26. Naomi W. Cohen, "Schools, Religion, and Government—Recent American Jewish Opinions," *Michael* 3 (1975): 343-44; cf. Murray Friedman, *The Utopian Dilemma* (Washington: Ethics & Public Policy Center, 1985), pp. 28-31.

Catholics had before them, that education in a religious setting benefited not only members of their own faith but also the nation as a whole, and that funds used to support secular studies at these schools should not be denied just because the schools happen to teach religious subjects on the side. They also cast doubt on the whole Jewish separationist approach to the problem of church and state, terming it "robot-like" and "unthinking."[27]

Major Jewish organizations were actually not quite as committed to the secularist agenda on church and state as their opponents imagined. Taxation of church property, elimination of chaplains from the public payroll, opposition to the phrase "In God We Trust," and related efforts to outlaw all manifestations of religion in American life never found significant support in Jewish quarters, probably because they failed to comport with Jewish interests that were, in the final analysis, not totally secular at all.[28] But these rarely talked about exceptions did not alter the overall thrust of Jewish rhetoric on the matter of church and state, much less Jewish policy on most issues of contemporary concern. In insisting that significant policy changes should take place, Orthodox Jews, later joined by neoconservatives and others, argued that the whole alliance with strict separationists should be abandoned. They sought in its stead a new partnership with groups laboring to shape government policy in a proreligion direction. They considered this—a position better rooted in American Jewry's past than they realized—to be in the best interests of Jews and Judaism, and good for interfaith relations as well. Where major Jewish organizations in the twentieth century feared erosion of the "no establishment" clause of the First Amendment, they stressed the need to champion "free exercise" of religion through laws and government programs designed to make it easier for observant Jews to uphold the tenets of their faith. To their way of thinking, the threat posed by rampant secularism was far more imminent and serious than any residual threat from the forces of militant Christianity.

4

The breakdown of the twentieth-century American Jewish consensus on the subject of church and state should not be surprising. If anything, the fact that the consensus lasted as long as it did is surprising, for it effectively masked an agonizing dilemma on the question of religion and state that characterizes much of modern Jewish history.

---

27. The words are those of Marvin Schick, quoted by Cohen in "Schools, Religion and Government," p. 377; cf. pp. 366-69.

28. See Yahalom, "American Judaism and the Question of Separation between Church and State," pp. 17-28.

On the one hand, history teaches Jews to favor strict church-state separation as the only defense against a Christian-dominated state. Those who emphasize this reading of history think that sooner or later "so-called non-denominational religious exercises" inevitably acquire "sectarian additions and deviations," and that "non-denominational" then becomes the majority's term for what the minority views as decidedly partisan. They fear that calls for religion in American life will, given the record of the past, likely turn into calls for a "Christian America." To prevent this, they argue for "a fence around the law so as to avoid approaches to transgression as well as actual transgression." They understandably worry that once religion gains entry into the public square, majority rule will trample minority rights, Christianizing everything in its path.[29]

On the other hand, history also teaches Jews to oppose secularization as a force leading to assimilation, social decay, and sometimes to persecution of all religions, Judaism included. Those who emphasize this reading of history welcome appropriate manifestations of religion in American life and propose a less absolutist approach to church-state separation—freedom *for* religion. They insist that "support for religion is basic to the American system" and fear that completely divorcing religion from national life will result in "a jungle where brute force, cunning, and unbridled passion rule supreme." Only the idea "that wrongdoing is an offense against the divine authority and order," they argue, can protect society against delinquency and crime. They also point out that Jews, as a small and often persecuted minority, should be wary of setting themselves too far apart from the majority, lest anti-Semitism result.[30]

What then of Jews in "Unsecular America"? They are caught between two positions, both of them historically legitimate, ideologically convincing, and fraught with dangers. Experience has taught Jews conflicting lessons, for those who have held aloft the banner of religion and those who have trampled down upon it have, at different times, proved both friendly and unfriendly. Jews, as idealists, may seek to promote a utopian society in America where they and their neighbors can live as equals, safe from the fire and brimstone of the Christian state *and* the desolate barrenness of the secular one. How best to realize such a society, however, remains an unsolved riddle.

---

29. Quoted material appears in Cohen, "Schools, Religion and Government," pp. 354, 345.

30. See Alvin I. Schiff, *The Jewish Day School in America* (New York: Jewish Education Committee Press, 1966), p. 177; and Cohen, "Schools, Religion and Government," p. 364.

Changing Christian Perceptions of Jews in America

Marvin R. Wilson

In a remote corner of the Egyptian Museum in Cairo stands a famous inscription. It is known as the Stele of Merneptah, a vital source for both biblical scholars and ancient historians.[1] On this slab, Pharaoh Merneptah (ca. 1220 B.C.) records a hymn of victory. It relates how he defeated the inhabitants of Palestine and Syria in a military campaign. Merneptah's inscription is important because it contains the oldest extrabiblical reference to Israel yet discovered. Concerning Israel the pharaoh brags, "Israel lies desolate; its seed is no more."

What a paradox! The great ancient civilization of the Egyptians—not to mention the Babylonians, Canaanites, and other nations of the Bible world—died more than two thousand years ago. Their dusty relics and ancient texts are preserved today in museums, mute testimony of once-thriving cultures now perished. Yet the Jewish people live. They now occupy their ancient homeland, and the Hebrew language—unlike hieroglyphics—is still alive and flourishing.

The mystery of the survival of the Jews and their ongoing importance to the world community has boggled some of the greatest minds of the ages. Voltaire once asked why the world should be made to rotate around the "insignificant pimple" of Jewry. Toynbee also had trouble coming to grips with the reality of contemporary Jewish life; he once stated that the Jew was merely a dried-up fossil, the vestige of a dead

---

1. See Jack Finegan, *Light from the Ancient Past: The Archaeological Background of Judaism and Christianity* (Princeton, N.J.: Princeton University Press, 1959), pp. 115-17.

culture. It would almost seem that Voltaire, Toynbee, and others like them really wanted to believe that Merneptah was right, that "Israel's seed is no more."

But as the world knows, Merneptah's words were neither historically accurate nor prophetic. Indeed, one of the certainties of this modern age is that Israel is real, Israel lives. God has been faithful. His words of promise to his elect have not failed. The Lord affirmed that he would make of Israel "a great nation" (Gen. 12:2), that his covenant would be "everlasting" (Gen. 17:7), and that Israel would be his people "for ever" (2 Sam. 7:24). Indeed, God's permanent pledge to Israel is as sure as his promise to uphold the fixed order of the sun, moon, and stars (Jer. 31:35-36).

Though modern Christians have been forced to acknowledge the fact of Jewish survival, many do not know how to interpret or respond to this phenomenon. For centuries, large segments of the church taught that Judaism is a dead and legalistic religion. It ceased to exist nearly two thousand years ago when the new covenant replaced the old. Judaism died and lost all theological relevance when Christianity, the second stage of the salvation rocket, took over. For the greater part of two millennia this belief has resulted in intense anger, pain, and conflict between church and synagogue. Relations between both communities remained largely gnarled and twisted because the history of the church is about as long as the history of anti-Semitism. Only in this century has there been any serious attempt to address this horrendous past record of Christian-Jewish relations.

Today there is abundant evidence that Christian perceptions of Jews have been undergoing intense reevaluation and change. Especially since the Second Vatican Counil (1963-65), great strides have been made in the field of interfaith relations. For a number of years prior to Vatican II, positive relations had been developing between the Jewish community and most mainline liberal Protestants. This rapprochement rather naturally came about due to a liberal stance on the part of both groups in economic, social-justice, and religious issues. In addition, Protestant documents issued by the World Council of Churches (e.g., Holland, 1948, and New Delhi, 1961) and statements by various church groups helped pave the way. In interreligious circles, the powerful influence of such Jewish leaders as Martin Buber, Abraham Heschel, and Marc Tanenbaum also did much to pioneer and further these Protestant-Jewish relations.

It has only been in the period after Vatican II, however, that significant progress has been made with both the Roman Catholic and fundamentalist/evangelical communities. The resulting dialogue has brought both Christian and Jewish participants to a new level of awareness and maturity about each other. In what follows, I will be giving an overview of how Christian perceptions of Jews have been changing rather than a detailed in-depth analysis of any particular area of change. It is my concern to highlight significant developments within various broad segments of the Christian community, though I will be focussing specially on the changing scene within the Roman Catholic Church and my own religious community, the evangelical church.

I. A STORMY PAST

The word *stormy* best describes the general climate of synagogue-church relations until the middle of this century. The cumulative effect of centuries of bad history between both communities makes the current thaw from this icy past an achievement little short of miraculous. For centuries immense barriers remained unscaled. Memories of ugly disputations needed healing. Painful myths and stereotypes awaited exploding.

Church and synagogue came to a parting of the ways toward the end of the first century. Since that time, wave after wave of hostility was directed by the church toward the Jew. The collective Jewish memory is long—understandably so—but unfortunately that of the Christian community is short. In this connection, Edward H. Flannery has pointed out in his recently revised work *The Anguish of the Jews* that "those pages of history Jews have committed to memory are the very ones that have been torn from Christian (and secular) history books."[2]

The church is just now beginning to come to grips with its past record of anti-Semitism. To this day the story of anti-Semitism and the church remains largely untold for it is often sordid. It contains many accounts of overt acts of hostility and hatred directed toward Jews as well as a record of guilty silences during those times when the Jewish community has been attacked by others—perhaps most scandalously during the Holocaust years. In this vein, Abraham Heschel wisely warns that "Indifference to evil is more insidious than evil itself; it is more universal, more contagious, more dangerous."[3]

One can appreciate the present change of climate in Christian-Jewish relations only by understanding the stormy history of past relations. A brief chronological survey of this tragic history is therefore in order. In this regard it must be stressed that much of the strife between Christians and Jews has centered on theological anti-Semitism promul-

---

2. Flannery, *The Anguish of the Jews*, rev. ed. (New York: Paulist Press, 1985), p. 1.

3. Heschel, "Religion and Race," in *The Insecurity of Freedom* (New York: Schocken Books, 1972), p. 92.

gated by the church. Christian literature and sermons have abounded with the preachment of contempt. Regrettably, New Testament teaching has been distorted and used as the basis of much of this error. The destruction of Jerusalem in the year 70 was said to be chastisement for Jewish rejection of Jesus' messianic claims. This event, which slaughtered, enslaved, and exiled hundreds of thousands of Jews, was held by some to be proof that God had forever cast away his once chosen people. It was taught that the Jews in their stubbornness and unbelief were no longer the people of God, that the church, the "new" and true Israel, had displaced the "old" Israel in the plan of God.

In the early Christian centuries an anti-Jewish polemic arose within the church. Leaders such as Justin Martyr, Ignatius of Antioch, and John Chrysostom spoke with great arrogance and derision against Jews and Judaism. Marcion, before the middle of the second century, sought to rid Christianity of every trace of Judaism: he attempted to remove the Old Testament from the canon of holy Scripture. Various church fathers also leveled the charge of deicide against the Jews. One of the first to do so was Melito of Sardis (120-185), who wrote, "God has been murdered, the King of Israel slain by an Israelite hand."[4] He was not only accusing the Jews of having murdered God by murdering Jesus but also suggesting that they ought to be held corporately culpable for this crime for all time. Hence Jews were forever consigned to bear misery and pain, a logical consequence of being disinherited from the grace of God. Called a "perverse people," Jews were denounced, cursed, and said to be possessed by the devil. The synagogue was described as a brothel, a place of robbers, and a den for evil beasts. Some Christians maintained that Christianity alone was spiritual and that Judaism was carnal because it represented a people rejected of God. In the pointed words of Augustine, "The Church admits and avows the Jewish people to be cursed, because after killing Christ they continue to till the ground of an earthly circumcision, an earthly Sabbath, an earthly Passover."[5]

By the Middle Ages, Jews were generally viewed as the outsiders of history, a wandering people condemned to suffer among the nations. Jews were accused of being a treacherous people, a pack of usurers, desecrators of the Host, murderers of Christian infants, spreaders of the Black Plague, poisoners of wells, and sucklers of sows.

The First Crusade was launched in 1096. In its wake came numerous forced baptisms, mass suicides, and burned synagogues. By 1215, the time of the Fourth Lateran Council (Pope Innocent III), Jews were

---

4. Melito of Sardis, quoted by Michael Rydelnik in "Who Are the Christ Killers?" *Moody Monthly*, October 1985, p. 38.

5. Augustine, quoted by Isaac Rottenberg in "Christians and Jews in Quiet Revolution," *Seventh Angel*, February 1985, p. 24.

ordered to wear distinctive clothes. Shortly after this, Jews began to be expelled from England, France, Spain, and other countries. The Spanish Inquisition and Expulsion of 1492 resulted in thousands of forced conversions, torturings, and burnings at the stake. Summing up hundreds of years of organized religious opposition against the Jew, Pinchas Lapide has noted that "No less than 96 church councils and 114 popes issued edicts against the Jews, mocking, scorning, disinheriting, and dispossessing them, treating them as pariahs, and bringing Israel to the brink of destruction."[6]

In the sixteenth century, Martin Luther produced a series of vitriolic pamphlets and addresses attacking Jews. He contemptuously referred to Jews as "thieves," "bitter worms," "thirsty bloodhounds," and "disgusting vermin"; he also called them "venomous," "stiffnecked," "ironheaded," and "stubborn as the devil."

The Jewish community emerged from the first half of the twentieth century decimated and perplexed. At the beginning of this century it had experienced a series of vicious pogroms in Russia that left thousands dead. More recently (1933-45), world Jewry endured the unspeakable horrors of the Holocaust, Hitler's so-called "final solution," which snuffed out six million Jews. In the years immediately following the Holocaust, Jews asked whether there was any place on this earth where they could peacefully live in security and freedom. Centuries of painful experience had taught them they could not depend on their "Christian" neighbors. But where else could they turn?

II. TOWARD A NEW CLIMATE

Many specialists in interfaith relations concur that in the past two decades more progress has been made in changing the attitudes of Christians toward Jews than took place in the previous 1900 years. The long history of hostility between younger and elder brother had created a fear and a lack of trust between both. The social isolation resulting from mutual alienation produced ignorance and negative stereotypes on both hands.

World War II, however, began to break down some of this separation. Christian GIs from all over America found themselves in the same units—and often in the same foxholes—with Jewish soldiers. Cooperation and social mixing brought about through military service was continued in a different context after the war. Recipients of the same GI bill of rights, Jews and Christians found themselves face-to-face in the classrooms of American colleges and universities. Furthermore, after the War, large numbers of Jewish people in America began moving from

---

6. Lapide, in *Jesus in Two Perspectives: A Jewish-Christian Dialog*, by Pinchas Lapide and Ulrich Luz (Minneapolis: Augsburg, 1985), p. 12.

their ethnocentric urban ghettos to the mainly Gentile suburbs. The new friendships afforded by these broadening social contacts created new opportunities for dissolving mistrust and superstition between Christians and Jews. The impact of Martin Buber's truism "All real living is meeting" was slowly becoming a reality.

In the years immediately following World War II the conscience of the world community began to be pricked as never before. Certainly news of the United Nations vote that led to the birth of the state of Israel was warmly greeted by the exhausted survivors of Hitler's madness. This small piece of real estate—the historic homeland of the Jews—became a welcome earthly haven. In Israel, Jews could now begin to shape their own destiny freely, no longer victims of those who sought their destruction. Israel also provided the opportunity for the further development of the Jewish religious and cultural identity. Contrary to the assertions of some, the state of Israel was not some sort of "atonement" on the part of the world for the Holocaust—nothing could serve that purpose. The fact of the matter is that progress toward the creation of a Jewish state was well underway even before the U.N. vote. Nevertheless, it is true that in the eyes of world Jewry, the creation of the state of Israel did seem to be a positive step toward righting an ugly historical wrong.

Although anti-Semitism in America did diminish during the 1950s and early sixties, it remained a significant problem. Prejudice against Jews was still felt in a number of key areas. Jews were still denied access to some resort hotels, homes in exclusive residential neighborhoods, country clubs, and civic clubs, and positions in industry. Dictionaries published during this period (as to the present day) continued to list the term *jew* as a verb meaning "to bargain sharply with; beat down in price." And the literature of various church and Sunday School groups perpetuated a number of negative stereotypes and caricatures of Jews reminiscent of the Middle Ages. But it would not be long before significant progress would be made on these and other issues.

Over the past two decades a number of important developments have contributed to the remarkably improved present climate in interfaith relations. Among Catholics, the work of Pope John XXIII in calling together the Ecumenical Council (Vatican II) has done more to eradicate Catholic-Jewish misperceptions than any other single force. Pope John knew of the pain of Jews under the Nazis from his period of service as apostolic delegate to Turkey, where he helped Jews escape. And he had been impressed by a visit in 1960 from the French Jewish historian Jules Isaac, who urged that church teaching on Jews and Judaism be corrected.[7] These experiences had a direct impact on the structuring of the Vatican II agenda.

---

7. See "Catholics and Jews: A New Rapprochement," *New York Times*, 20 October 1985, p. 40.

In section four of the 1965 Vatican II decree "Declaration on Relations with Non-Christians," issued by Pope Paul VI (Pope John's successor), many important affirmations and corrections were offered. In this document, often referred to as *Nostra Aetate* ("In Our Times"), the church's Jewish ancestry and spiritual debt to Judaism is freely acknowledged. The document states that although "the Church is the new people of God, the Jews should not be presented as rejected and accursed of God." Concerning the death of Jesus it states, "what happened in Christ's passion cannot be charged against all Jews, then alive without distinction, nor against the Jews of today." Furthermore, this Vatican II statement stresses that "the Church decries hatred, persecution, and displays of anti-Semitism directed against Jews at any time and by anyone." In addition, in light of the church's common spiritual roots with the Jewish community, the document states that "the Council recommends and wishes to foster understanding and respect from Biblical and theological studies and from fraternal dialogue." Today the Vatican has an office for Catholic-Jewish relations to encourage further contact and understanding between both communities.

Before the end of the sixties, the Archdiocese of New York in consultation with Jewish community leaders issued a document entitled "Guidelines for the Advancement of Catholic-Jewish Relations." This valuable statement called for studying the New Testament in its Jewish setting, reexamining pharisaism at the time of Jesus, avoiding proselytizing as part of dialogue, repudiating anti-Semitic statements in textbooks, and affirming the permanency of God's election and covenant with Israel despite the election of Christianity. In the years following, other diocesan offices—including Houston, Los Angeles, Cleveland, and Detroit— have also issued their own guidelines for improving Catholic-Jewish relations. Furthermore, the Catholic Church maintains the office of the U.S. Secretariat for Catholic-Jewish Relations in Washington, D.C. Through this office and other diocesan offices, much progress has been made in furthering Catholic-Jewish understanding. In the recent words of Cardinal Joseph Bernadin, Christian doctrine needs to be stated "in such a way as to acknowledge authentic theological space for Judaism." Religious and Holocaust curricula have been written with this acknowledgment in mind. A Passover Hagaddah has been adapted in order to let Catholics celebrate the seder with their Jewish friends. In addition, many Catholic universities offer courses on Judaism and the Jewish people. The general result has been summed up most positively by one international Jewish spokesperson: "During the past two decades, 'a revolution in mutual esteem' has taken place between millions of Catholics and Jews throughout the world."[8]

---

8. "Rabbi Sees Improved Ties with Christians," U.P.I. story in the

Similar progress, especially since the late sixties, may also be charted between evangelicals and Jews. By the mid-seventies Martin E. Marty had observed that the deepening of evangelical-Jewish relations in this country and in regard to Israel was "the most significant religious trend in the United States."[9]

One of the strong motivations on the part of evangelicals to enter into dialogue with Jews is a genuine interest in deepening their understanding of the Jewish roots of the Christian faith. Evangelicals are a people strongly wed to the biblical text. Rabbi Joshua Haberman is correct in noting that "the Bible, far more than any kind of opportunistic political alliance, is the abiding ground on which evangelical-Jewish relations will grow."[10] In the forties, with the founding of such organizations as the National Association of Evangelicals (1942), Fuller Theological Seminary (1947), and the Evangelical Theological Society (1949), a "new evangelicalism" began to appear. Far less anti-intellectual and separatistic than its fundamentalist forebears, evangelicalism emerged into the fifties and sixties with increased cultural openness and interest in pursuing ecumenical dialogue. This openness led a number of younger evangelicals to begin pursuing graduate work in the fields of Hebrew and Judaic Studies. At Jewish institutions such as Dropsie College, Brandeis University, and Hebrew Union College, Jewish professors such as Cyrus Gordon and Samuel Sandmel served as mentors to a coterie of evangelical scholars. Many of these graduates now teach in evangelical colleges and seminaries, and one, the late G. Douglas Young, a Dropsie College graduate, founded the Institute for Holy Land Studies in Jerusalem, which now has formal ties with more than a hundred evangelical schools of higher learning. Evangelicals who have studied under Jewish scholars are currently one of the strongest forces in America geared to promoting positive and intelligent dialogue with the Jewish community. Motivated by a desire to understand the Hebraic message and background of the Bible, these people are fully appreciative of the benefits they have received from having had the opportunity to discuss the Scriptures face-to-face with the people whose ancestors produced the book.

A second factor that has contributed to a more positive climate for dialogue is the growing impact of relational theology within evangelicalism. Today evangelicals are seeking to balance the doctrinal and propositional side of truth with its relational and personal dimension. Evangelicals are learning the importance of relating to others first and foremost as people, not as mere trophies to be targeted and bagged on an

---

Beverly (Mass.) Times, 24 November 1984, p. A7.

9. Marty, Context, 1 January 1978, p. 1.

10. Haberman, "The Ties That Bind," United Evangelical Action, July-August 1983, p. 7.

evangelistic safari. Evangelicals have not always been sensitive in their outreach to others. Instead of creating a positive interest on the part of others through their lifestyle and witness (see Rom. 11:11), they have sometimes succumbed to an evangelical zeal marked by insensitivity and ignorance that has produced the opposite effect. Evangelicals are now discovering that lasting friendships with Jewish people are built on mutual trust. They are learning that their first step must be to earn this sort trust as well as the right to be heard. Indeed, many evangelicals are coming to realize that their friendship, respect, and care for Jewish people—and for all people—should be unconditional, genuine, and irrevocable, never preconditioned or governed by the acceptance of any Christian belief or dogma.

Another factor that has helped foster evangelical-Jewish dialogue is the curiosity on the part of Jews about the religious commitment of evangelicals holding high public office and the parallel impact of the new Christian Right. Jimmy Carter began his drive to the presidency in 1975 as a "born-again" Christian. Jews immediately became curious about the religious background of this southern evangelical. The same curiosity was again piqued in the mid-eighties when religious broadcaster M. G. "Pat" Robertson declared that he was pondering a bid for the presidency. Many Jews have questions about such a prospect. "How would a self-professed born-again Christian lead a pluralistic nation of more than two hundred million?" "Would he be a president who is evangelical or would he prove to be an evangelical president?" "If the latter, what effect would this have on Jews and all other Americans who for centuries have prized the priceless right of religious liberty?" In addition, with the rise of the new Christian Right, Jews have been asking whether it is the goal of organizations like the Moral Majority to create a "Christian republic" by "Christianizing" government and politics. Since many affiliated with the new Christian Right claim either an evangelical or fundamentalist religious identity, interfaith dialogue has been providing a useful platform to air these and other issues.

A fourth reason prompting greater evangelical-Jewish contact is the jointly perceived need to dispel faulty images and popular stereotypes of each other. Both groups freely acknowledge that many prejudices, distortions, and faulty perceptions exist. The geographical concentration of evangelicals is largely in the South and the "Bible belt" of the Midwest. Jews, on the other hand, are located mostly in the Northeast and large cities of the West. Various half-truths and stereotypical images arise from this mutual isolation—"Elmer Gantrys," "rednecks," and "wild-eyed religious fanatics" on the one hand, and "Pharisees," "Shylocks," and "people whose prayers God doesn't hear" on the other. Today, a new climate in interfaith relations has provided a platform for personal encounters that are dissolving these regrettable stereotypes and uncovering more accurate portraits. Evangelicals are coming to realize that Judaism has developed through the centuries, that it is not simply the blood-sacrifice religion of the Old Testament. Jews are coming to see that not all evangelicals are simple "street preacher" types, interested solely in personal redemption, that evangelicals too can be enlivened by a real passion for justice.

These are only some of the factors and motives that lie behind the current evangelical-Jewish encounter. Others include a common interest in the security and survival of the state of Israel, a greater ecumenical and minority-group consciousness brought about by the civil rights movement and specialized efforts aimed at easing racial tensions, mutual concern to secure human rights—especially freedom—for those Jews and Christians trapped in the Soviet Union, a realization of the need within both communities for education about the Holocaust, and a deeply felt need among evangelicals especially to address and right various historical wrongs committed in the name of the Christian faith. [11]

As this century draws rapidly to a close, it becomes increasingly evident how far we have moved toward a new climate of maturity in Christian-Jewish dialogue. The immense problems of the past that brought separation and acrimony between the two communities are now being addressed with candor and are being resolved. Christians and Jews are coming to see each other no longer as enemies but as allies, jointly called to witness to God in an increasingly secular society. There are still disagreements, but they are being handled more and more as family disputes. But more importantly, beneath it all there is a mutual respect and growing commitment to each other not present twenty years ago.

III. PRESENT WINDS OF CHANGE

The new climate of openness and personal encounter that has developed since the mid-sixties has resulted in many changes in the way Christians perceive Jews and Judaism. In many areas lay people are just now becoming aware of issues that religious leaders and clergy have been grappling with for several decades. This is not unusual. In movements of religious reform, the full impact of change is often not felt at the grass-roots level until years after scholars and professionals have thoroughly discussed and written about them. In this third main section of my essay I will briefly

---

11. For a more extensive discussion of factors stimulating the current evangelical-Jewish encounter, see my articles "An Evangelical View of the Current State of Evangelical-Jewish Relations," *Journal of the Evangelical Theological Society*, June 1982, pp. 139-60; and "Evangelicals and Jews Are Talking," *Christian Herald*, May 1981, pp. 26-28, 52, 53, 58.

survey some additional areas in which Christians are coming to grips with change in regard to the Jewish community.

First, there is the area of anti-Semitism and Holocaust education. It is very clear that a greater effort is being made today to educate Christians about anti-Semitism and the Holocaust. Many public schools have adopted the recent *Facing History and Ourselves* curriculum on the Holocaust and genocide. [12] More than twenty-five percent of Catholic high schools now use some form of Holocaust education in their curricula. In 1985 the Vatican issued a document entitled "Notes on the Correct Way to Present Jews and Judaism in Preaching and Catechesis in the Roman Catholic Church." Though this document has drawn criticism from the Jewish community for failing to emphasize the moral challenge that the Holocaust poses for the Christian community, it is nonetheless representative of ongoing efforts to implement the teachings of Vatican II in a practical manner.

Holocaust education will remain a growing concern in interfaith circles in the decades ahead. David Wyman, author of the well-known volume *The Abandonment of the Jews*, has demonstrated the great need among Christians for this education. He has stressed that the Holocaust "is still not perceived by non-Jews as their issue—or their loss." He further emphasizes that the Holocaust was a "Christian tragedy" by pointing out that "It was Christians who perpetrated it—the Nazis who were the product of Western Christian civilization and those Christians in the U.S. and Britain who stood by and failed in their Christian duty to do everything to stop it and to help those who needed help." [13]

While revisionist historians continue to question whether the Holocaust really happened and neo-Nazi hate groups distribute their literature throughout the land, not everyone in the church today is silent. In the summer of 1985, a group of fifteen clergy from various denominations in the Boston area spontaneously came together to form a Christian Clergy Task Force on Anti-Semitism. This interdenominational ministerial group is one of the first to be organized in the country for the purpose of meeting regularly to become informed about anti-Semitism

---

12. The Facing History and Ourselves National Foundation, Inc., is committed to helping teachers and administrators bring education about twentieth-century genocide, specifically the Holocaust and the genocide of the Armenian people, to students and their communities. The program uses the resource book *Facing History and Ourselves: Holocaust and Human Behavior*, and the Foundation provides numerous services and resources including a regular newsletter. For further information, write to Facing History and Ourselves, 25 Kennard Rd., Brookline, Massachusetts 02146.

13. Wyman, interviewed by Aviva Cantor in "The Holocaust—Also a Christian Tragedy," *Jewish Advocate*, March 1985, p. 12.

and mobilizing during times of crisis to take appropriate action in response to any anti-Semitic incidents. The Task Force believes that Christians everywhere must ever remain vigilant and be prepared to speak out against this ubiquitous evil.

Another positive development in the war to combat anti-Semitism is the work being done cooperatively by Christians and Jews to change the Oberammergau Passion Play. When I saw the play in 1984 during its 350th anniversary season, I was impressed by its power, but I was disappointed by its anti-Semitic slant. Though the text of the play was revised for the 1980 production, and again for 1984, it still perpetuated the myth that Jews collectively, then and now, must bear the guilt of Jesus' crucifixion. Furthermore, Jews are portrayed as corrupt, bloodthirsty antagonists, and Jewish law is represented as cruel and vindictive. Jewish authorities are dressed in strange costumes with horned hats, while Jesus and his followers are clad in simple flowing robes. The play also fails to emphasize Jesus' positive identity with his first-century Jewish roots. Along with this, a questionable selection of passages from the Gospels allows Jesus' Jewish contemporaries to come across as the villains of the play, while those guilty of Roman oppression are virtually ignored.

Numerous articles and reviews of the Oberammergau play and of the teaching of other current Passion plays have appeared in recent years. Several detailed critiques recommending specific changes in the text of the Oberammergau play have also been published. The National Conference of Christians and Jews and other concerned groups have produced useful materials dealing with the Passion narratives.

Each time the village of Oberammergau produces this Passion play (normally once a decade), more than half a million people come to view it from around the world. Sadly, most spectators who have been asked about the play indicate that they think it is an accurate and faithful portrayal of the story of Jesus. Considerable work obviously still needs to be done before the next scheduled Oberammergau performance in 1990. Unfortunately, however, the removal of anti-Semitism—wherever it is found—is a very slow process that requires persistence and patience. As Edward Flannery realistically reminds us in his survey of the current scene, "Antisemitism is not in its death throes. A civilization contaminated so long with a toxin so virulent could hardly be detoxified in such short order."[14] But if Catholic reforms in the annual Passion week liturgy have already led from praying for the "perfidious Jews" to praying for the "conversion of the Jews" to praying that Jewish people may be faithful to their covenant, we have reason to hope that some future day will also bring changes in the Oberammergau production.

---

14. Flannery, *The Anguish of the Jews*, p. 283.

Changes in Christian perceptions of Jews are also becoming evident in theology. For centuries the church taught that Jews have no continuing covenant with God, that the history of Israel came to an end with Jesus. The church took the place of God's ancient people with its "new" covenant. As J. Coert Rylaarsdam has put it, this had the effect of making Judaism the Christian problem: "In making his inevitable definition of the Jew the Christian has assumed that because his own faith is 'true' that of the Jew can be true no longer. That is his problem."[15]

Many Christian theologians have attempted of late to produce a revisionist theology of Judaism. In an effort to establish the theological validity of Judaism, considerable time has been spent reworking and emending various passages from the New Testament thought to be anti-Judaic in teaching. By rethinking traditional Christology, many revisionists have accepted a "two covenant" theory, a concept earlier expounded by Jewish scholar Franz Rosenzweig (1886-1929). In short, this view teaches that Judaism has been with God the Father from the very beginning. Judaism does not need to be converted, since its pilgrimage to God has already been completed. Non-Jews, however, need the Son in order to come to the Father. The vocation of Christians therefore is to bring the rest of humanity to God through Christianity. Though Paul Van Buren's observation may be correct that "Now, the main body of Christians believes God's covenant with the Jews is still in effect and will endure forever,"[16] not every Christian is comfortable with the kind of Christological revision often demanded by the ecumenical broad-mindedness of some dialogue. More conservative Christians have usually questioned the wisdom of Christological revision out of a concern that it might impair the uniqueness of Christianity. Other Christians have taken issue with Rosemary Ruether's claim that anti-Semitism is the "left hand of Christology."

We can also find evidence of how theological thinking about Jews is changing in the furor that arose in 1980 when the president of the Southern Baptists stated from the pulpit of a large evangelical church in Oklahoma that "God Almighty does not hear the prayer of a Jew." Jews and Christians alike immediately jumped into the heated debate that followed. Many Christians found these remarks insensitive at best and offensive and arrogant at worst. Others expressed concern that the statement would undercut respect and appreciation for Jews and Judaism and that if left unchecked they might ultimately pave the way for a new wave of anti-Semitism. After the evangelical leader who had made the state-

---

15. Rylaarsdam, "Judaism: The Christian Problem," *Face to Face*, Spring 1984, p. 4.

16. Quoted in *Context*, 1 and 15 August 1983, p. 2.

ment met with Jewish leaders (even taking a tour of Israel with them), he offered an apology, and the controversy subsided. Following a meeting of his own with a national Jewish leader, the Rev. Jerry Falwell made a comment with regard to the whole incident that in its simplicity struck a more immediately responsive chord among many American Christians: "God hears the cry of any sincere person who calls on him."

A greater awareness of Jewish sensitivities is also now being observed in the use of certain Christian terminology. A growing number of Christians choose to refer to the Old Testament as the "First" or "Original" Testament, or simply the "Jewish" or "Hebrew Scriptures." Also, many are coming to view such things as the law-versus-love distinction between the testaments and the common equating of "Pharisee" with "hypocrite" as misleading and invalid. And in many public school classrooms the use of Christmas carols—many of which have overtly Christocentric wording—is being rethought. Increased learning by Christians about Hanukkah, a Jewish holiday commemorating religious freedom (a festival that Jesus himself celebrated—see John 10:22), has resulted in Hanukkah songs being introduced into classrooms with increasing frequency.

As Christians reexamine their understanding of theological literature, Jews are making efforts to understand Christianity more accurately through a study of its original sources. In the words of New Testament scholar Rabbi Michael Greenwald, "To many Jews, a Jew who studies the New Testament is an apostate; a rabbi who does so is eccentric."[17] Yet Jewish scholar Ellis Rivkin points to the essential Jewishness of the New Testament, arguing that the document is a "mutation-revelation within Judaism."[18] The great Maimonides encouraged dialogue with Christians, pointing out that no harm will come since "They will not find in their Torah [the Christian Bible] anything that conflicts with our Torah."[19] David Flusser of the Hebrew University in Jerusalem and other Jewish scholars have likewise noted the profound Jewishness of most of the New Testament narratives. There is a greater openness on the part of Jews today to study the New Testament. Various temples and Jewish education programs are now providing courses in such study, efforts in which local Christian clergy occasionally assist. The Jewish

17. Greenwald, "When a Rabbi Studies the New Testament," *Genesis 2*, April 1985, p. 13.

18. Rivkin, "A Jewish View of the New Testament," in *Evangelicals and Jews in an Age of Pluralism*, ed. Marc H. Tanenbaum, Marvin R. Wilson, and A. James Rudin (Grand Rapids: Baker, 1984), p. 101.

19. Maimonides, quoted by Harvey Falk in *Jesus the Pharisee: A New Look at the Jewishness of Jesus* (New York: Paulist Press, 1985), p. 4.

Anti-Defamation League and the Roman Catholic Archdiocese of Philadelphia are working together to prepare a booklet that will introduce Jews
to the basic teachings and history of Christianity.

A third realm in which Christian perspectives on Jews are being
rethought is that of evangelistic outreach. On this point the Jewish position is clear: Christian missionary activity directed toward Jews is a threat
to Jewish survival; if unchecked, it may lead to cultural genocide.

Since Vatican II, Christians have been much more inclined to
listen to Jews define themselves, and this has significantly affected their
understanding of outreach to Jews. Roger Cardinal Etchegaray, Arch-
bishop of Marseilles, recently said that "As long as Christianity has not
integrated Judaism in its history of salvation there are always seeds of anti-
Semitism that can be reborn." Since Bible times, Christians have sent
basically one message to Jews: "You have everything to learn from us; we
have no reason to listen to you." Today, however, things are changing.
Former president of the Synagogue Council of America Mordecai Waxman has observed a new trend: "For the first time in 2,000 years, Christianity is prepared to listen to Jews on their own terms."[20]

Christian mission specially aimed at Jews has been undergoing
reassessment and change. For the Jewish community, fundamentalists
and evangelicals—not liberal Protestants or Catholics—have posed particular problems in regard to missionary campaigns. This has created a
Jewish dilemma: do Jews accept the strong political support that evangelicals offer them in regard to Israel while overlooking their reluctance
to allow Jews the right of full theological self-definition? Or do Jews opt
for closer ties with those within the Christian community who exert little
or no missionary zeal regarding them and yet whose support of Israel has
at best been questionable?

In recent years evangelicals and fundamentalists have been taking a
second look at missionary principles and practices. As a result, a number
of leaders are now taking a clear stand against singling out Jews as some
uniquely needy objects for proselytism. Evangelist Billy Graham has
stated, "In my evangelical efforts I have never been called to single out
Jews as Jews. . . . God has always had a special relationship with the
Jewish people."[21] Jerry Falwell has said he does not believe the New
Testament teaches that Christians are "to zero in on anybody" and that
those who do believe this "are missing the commission of the Christian
Gospel, which is to preach to everyone."[22] Others from the conservative

20. "Waxman Promotes Spirit of Cooperation," U.P.I. interview in the
Beverly (Mass.) Times, 7 September 1985, p. A8.
    21. Graham, quoted by Leo Trepp in *Judaism: Development and Life,*
3rd ed. (Belmont, Cal.: Wadsworth, 1982), p. 183.
    22. Falwell, quoted by Merrill Simon in *Jerry Falwell and the Jews*

Christian community now denounce "hard-line conversionary tactics" and dissociate themselves from deceptive, devious, coercive, and manipulative evangelistic methods. Currently the evangelical community is struggling with what it means for an evangelical to be genuinely "evangelical"—that is, faithful to tradition and the historic Christian call to spread the gospel to all men (Matt. 28:18-20; Acts 1:8) and yet do so in an honest, open, and humble way.

Evangelicals are coming to realize that Christians are not called to convert anyone. Conversion is God's work, not man's. The history of the church indicates that Christians have often sought to show their love for the Jewish people by trying to convert them. Unfortunately, such blood-shrouded events as the Crusades and the Inquisition bear painful testimony that tens of thousands of Jews were "loved" to death in the name of Christ. Jewish leader Yechiel Eckstein has sought to help the evangelical community by pointing out a better way. He has stressed to evangelicals that Jewish survival is the central force guiding Jewish life today, while for evangelicals it is the proclamation of the gospel to the world. Though there is a conflict between the core self-definitions of the two communities, Eckstein says that evangelical-Jewish relations need not be doomed to failure. I agree. But, as Eckstein stresses, both communities will need to build a *modus vivendi* that will allow each to affirm its own central commission in a way least offensive to the other.[23]

The messianic Jewish movement poses a growing challenge for both Jews and Christians. Much of the financial backing for messianic or Jewish Christian congregations and missions comes from fundamentalist and mainline evangelical churches. Their supporters recognize them not as fringe groups or cults made up of religious fanatics but as those who represent a legitimate outgrowth of early Christianity.

The Jewish community, however, is generally unwilling to acknowledge that Jews can believe in Jesus as Messiah and still rightfully retain their Jewish identity. Jews cannot have it both ways; they must choose on what side of the fence they will fall—Jewish or Christian. Some Jewish leaders today urge fundamentalist and evangelical churches not to support the Jewish-Christian cause on the grounds that it is little more than a fraud. Evangelicals often counter by arguing that Jewish Christianity is "biblical" and hence authentic, and that according to Jewish law there is nothing a Jew can ever believe or do that can take away from the fact of his or her Jewishness, which is established by birth. A Jew may be lapsed or errant, they argue, but he or she is still a Jew.

(Middle Village, N.Y.: Jonathan David, 1984), p. 35. See also "An Era of Understanding," *Boston Globe*, 5 April 1985, p. 2.

23. See Eckstein, *What Christians Should Know about Jews and Judaism* (Waco, Tex.: Word Books, 1984), pp. 320-21.

Presently, many evangelicals feel caught in a vise regarding messianic Jews. They feel they are being forced to choose sides—either to support the Jewish community by seeking to negate or ostracize messianic Jews, many of whom are Christian friends, or to support the Christian community in affirming the legitimacy of the messianic movement, and by doing so run the risk of alienating their Jewish friends. Unfortunately, the complex problem of Jewish Christianity has not yet been thoroughly addressed by the interfaith movement today. Ignoring this troublesome phenomenon will not cause it to go away. Indeed, should deeply agitated Christians ever start to direct anger and hostility toward Jews who seek to discredit other Jews for believing in Jesus, it may eventually cause a backlash that will destroy some of the gains already made in interfaith relations.

A fourth area in which Christians are changing their perceptions of Jews involves the state of Israel. Of all Christian groups, evangelicals and fundamentalists have been the strongest supporters of Israel. This has been primarily due to their literalness of biblical interpretation and their belief in predictive prophecy concerning the return of Israel to the land. A current practical outworking of this approach to Scripture was reported in a recent major story in the *Wall Street Journal* about evangelical business executives who are investing millions in a project that uses the Bible to search for oil in Israel. Until recent times, many evangelicals have seen Israel chiefly in theological terms and have given their support primarily for theological reasons. Many maintain that Israel has a "divine right" to the land, and they view the return of Jews to the land as a prelude to Jesus' Second Coming.[24] Some stress the need for conversion of the Jews to Christianity before that coming.

One recent positive effect of evangelical-Jewish dialogue is that evangelicals are coming to see Israel as far more than part of some apocalyptic theological scenario. Israel is no longer being viewed simplistically as the key piece in God's gigantic eschatological jigsaw puzzle. Rather, Israel is being understood by a growing number of evangelicals as a contemporary nation-state struggling for long-term survival. It deserves their support not simply for biblical and historical reasons but for social-justice, humanitarian, and ethical reasons as well. Furthermore, evangelicals are freer today to criticize specific political policies or military actions of the Israelis without fear of being labeled "anti-Zionist" or "anti-Semitic." They are giving evidence of a growing concern for legitimate Palestinian rights, which would seem to reflect a growing realization that God is on the side of justice and has love for all people.

---

24. This 1985 *Journal* story by George Getschow, entitled "Evangelicals Use Bible to Track Oil in Israel," was reprinted in *The Boston Jewish Times*, 29 August 1985, pp. 1, 11.

Evangelical missionary work in the Arab world, however, continues to pose a special problem for those who choose to lend encouragement to the Zionist cause. Nonetheless, evangelicals are more and more coming to the position that to be "pro-Arab" does not have to mean "anti-Israel" any more than being "pro-Israel" must mean "anti-Arab." In short, there is a growing evangelical concern that American Christians must work to establish a just and creative sharing of the land between both peoples.

Evangelical support for Israel is not waning but rather maturing. Evangelicals are far less apt to express unconditional support for Israel today than they once were. Their approach to Israel is becoming increasingly thoughtful. There are reasons for this change. One pertains to the 1982-85 incursion of Israel into Lebanon. This war may have brought Israel's security problem to the world's attention, but it also threw a spotlight on the plight of the Palestinian people and raised many questions raised about the wisdom of Israeli foreign policy and related issues. Should Israel have authorized the bombing of a PLO base in North Africa, more than a thousand miles to the west of Israel? How can Rabbi Meir Kahane's racist policies, which are endorsed by thousands of Israeli Jews, be squared with Moses' teaching that one must be compassionate and just in dealing with one's neighbor in the land? How is it that the Israelis can work so closely with the U.S. (receiving more than two billion dollars in American aid annually) and yet engage in espionage against their benefactors, as in the case of Jonathan Pollard, a Navy counterintelligence analyst who in 1985 was arrested and charged with spying on the United States and selling top-secret information to Israel. Despite these and other questions, it seems likely that because evangelical support of Israel remains firmly rooted in biblical teaching rather than politics, evangelicals will continue to remain true friends of Israel in the years ahead.

Unlike evangelicals, the Catholic Church in general has not experienced such positive relations with the Jewish community regarding Israel. This has been mainly due to the hesitancy of the Catholic Church to establish formal and full diplomatic relations with the Jewish state. The Vatican has offered several reasons for its refusal to grant de jure recognition to Israel: the ambiguity over the borders of the West Bank and the status of Jerusalem, the need to protect the rights of Palestinians, and concern about what Christians in Arab countries might suffer should Israel be formally recognized. Arthur Hertzberg, however, is correct in arguing that dialogue between Jews and Catholic cannot succeed unless it addresses the temporal concerns of both communities. The failure of Rome to recognize Israel, he believes, is symptomatic: "Church leaders refuse to accept the notion that world Jewry—like the Church itself—has temporal as well as spiritual concerns. They want to treat us as a purely spiritual entity so they can avoid dealing with the issue that matters most to us—explicit recognition of Israel."[25] An increasing number of Catholic leaders feel that the Vatican position must change regarding Israel. Until that occurs, however, Israel will likely remain a sticking point in Catholic-Jewish relations.

IV. CHRISTIAN REPENTANCE: KEY TO FUTURE CHANGE

For nearly two thousand years the church has said to the Jew, "You repent!" But as regards the Jew, the church itself has never seriously come to grips with the need for its own repentance. A spirit of hubris has kept the church from facing its own sin and constituted a major impediment in the history of Christian-Jewish relations. The church must change, and Christian repentance is the key. Only when the church gets its own spiritual house in order can there be any long-term optimism about the future of Christian-Jewish relations.

For decades theologians and sociologists have argued that the best way to deal with anti-Semitism is through education. But education alone is not the answer. Many of Hitler's notorious SS men held the Ph.D. degree from European universities and were churchmen as well, yet they acted like barbarians, lacking all compassion for their fellow humanity. The human soul cannot be effectively changed from the outside; there must be something that penetrates deeply to effect a change from the inside out. That deeper work is repentance.

Dietrich Bonhoeffer once stated that repentance is the key to the health of the church. Indeed, the church cannot hope to be fully healed of its sickness concerning the Jew unless it first deals with the issue of repentance.

The Hebrew word for repentance, *teshuvah,* literally means "returning" or "going back." In the Bible it often connotes God's convicting work whereby a person turns aside from sin and returns to God in faith and renewal. But *teshuvah* may also be translated "response" or "answer." God is always talking to people, but they are not always listening. When they respond to the voice and promptings of God's Spirit within, repentance begins to take place; a change is begun. This idea of repentance as change is reflected in the New Testament Greek term *metanoia,* meaning literally "to change the mind." This change is not humanly contrived; it is not the product of mere psychological manipulation; it is more than an emotional feeling. Repentance comes when God convicts us of our sin. It is not a once-and-for-all event. In the words of the contemporary rabbinic scholar Adin Steinsaltz, "Repentance is a stage

---

25. Hertzberg, "Rome Must Recognize Israel," *New York Times* 4 December 1985, p. A31.

on an everlasting journey." It is a process, a prayer that is lived daily; it is a turning point that must be reached over and over again. Rabbinic literature places special emphasis on this point: "Rabbi Eleazar said: 'Repent one day before your death.' His disciples asked him, 'Who knows when he will die?' Rabbi Eleazar answered, 'All the more then should a man repent today, for he might die tomorrow. The result of this will be that all his life will be spent in repentance'" (Midrash Tehillim 90:16).

Anti-Semitism is a spiritual problem and requires a spiritual solution, repentance. It is a spiritual problem because anti-Semitism is rooted in the pride that denies God's sovereignty in choosing the Jew. The Lord chose Israel "out of all the peoples on the face of the earth to be his people, his treasured possession" (Deut. 7:6). Whenever the church has sought to negate the "apple of God's eye," a unique people chosen to be the vehicle of revelation and blessing to the world (Gen. 12:3), it has violated the authority of God. Anti-Semitism is an affront to God's will because it denies his wisdom and calling. It is an arrogant rejection of the notion that God's covenant with Israel is eternal. It is the casting aside of one's elder brother. It is an attempt by the "wild branches" to usurp the place of the roots and trunk of the cultivated olive tree (cf. Rom. 11:17-24). Only when God's love is allowed to change the bitterness and hostility of human hearts through repentance will anti-Semitism fully cease.

It is imperative that the church realize that Israel's election does not entail spiritual superiority or exclusive possession of innate gifts. The Jewish community has understood chosenness as a summons to action, a call to responsibility, an acceptance of the burden of Torah. And, on the other hand, when Christians affirm Jewish chosenness, they must not fall into the trap of seeking to idealize Jewish people. Christians must learn to accept actual Jews—as they are now, on their sin-prone human level. They must not look for an idealized Jew on an other-worldly, not-yet-existent spiritual level. Jews seek to be understood as people in a relationship of mutuality. They have never desired as a people to be viewed as objects "on a pedestal" or those specially loved.

The church is called to function as a body, each member of the body bearing responsibility for the other. The church is not made up of independent individuals who have no relation to other parts of the body. There is a corporate solidarity. When one part of the body suffers, all parts suffer, the whole body is affected. All are members one of another. It is futile to try to dissociate oneself from the rest of the body. All members bear responsibility for the weaknesses and strengths of each other. In this connection, it is often claimed that the victimizers and bystanders of the Holocaust were not *genuine* Christians, but "Christians" in name only. But this line of reasoning is both shaky and fallacious. One cannot avoid the fact that most of these people were baptized, church-going Christians. If fundamentalist, "Bible-believing" Christians in America are capable of bombing abortion clinics, is the thought of Christian collaboration in the Holocaust any less believable? Who is to say how "evil" it is possible for Christians to be in their actions? If the church is a worldwide fellowship, then Christian repentance must also be a catholic concern.

According to Maimonides, the process of repentance involves four steps. First there is confession, the frank acknowledgment of one's failure. In this connection, the church today has a poor sense of historical awareness. In most churches there is little knowledge of the history of anti-Semitism and the Holocaust. When there is historical awareness it is possible to deal with the spiritual necessity of repentance. Guilt paralyzes one from action, but the gospel makes one free. One cannot repent for others, but one can deplore what others have done. Repentance is not just for the wicked; we must all be concerned with the quality of our attitudes and actions so they can be raised to a higher level. Certainly the Holocaust shows the silence, indifference, and failure of man to be his brother's keeper. The Sermon on the Mount underscores the importance of coming to terms quickly with one's brother. "If you are offering your gift at the altar and there remember that your brother has something against you, leave your gift there in front of the altar. First go and be reconciled to your brother; then come and offer your gift" (Matt. 5:23-24).

Following confession, as a second step, there must be sorrow and regret over the wrong that has been done. Third, the act of repentance involves a resolve not to repeat the sin again. Godly repentance entails being sorry enough to quit. The final step in the process of repentance is reconciliation and restoration, turning from the ugliness of the past and joy at the thought of a new beginning. With reconciliation comes the fruit of repentance. These deeds will be directed to those who have been sinned against, thus giving evidence of the sincerity of the act. Since the church was silent when Jews were being destroyed in the past, today it is only reasonable that it be incumbent upon the church to provide support for Israel. This concrete step of social action to effect restoration is crucial. Otherwise the concept of repentance will amount to little more than pious-sounding theological rhetoric.

Abraham Heschel once said that a prophet is a man who knows what time it is. Recent years have brought a climate of openness and revolutionary changes in interfaith relations. The significance of these sorts of changes in the future, and the speed with which they will continue to take place, will depend on the willingness of the church to effect a new relationship with the Jewish community through the dynamic of repentance. The hour has come. Does the church know what time it is?

American Jews and America: The Mission of Israel Revisited

David Novak

I

An American Jew can see his or her relationship to America in one of four ways, and which of these four ways is assigned prime importance ultimately reveals how that Jew is related to Judaism itself.

1. Some American Jews see their relationship to America in essentially juridical terms—that is, they see themselves as the anonymous legal personalities who are the subjects of the law of this democracy. Many of these Jews have served as leaders of other Americans who resist any emphasis on the interests of subgroups ("hyphenated Americans") in American public life. For them, America is still the melting pot that is supposed to create but one enduring public realm, devoid of "special interests."[1] For all such Americans, this public realm is the primary source of human values.

These Jews never think of Judaism as more than a denomination of like-minded individuals, and many have eliminated it from their lives altogether. Those who have not eliminated Judaism from their lives have

I want to thank the following friends with whom I discussed various point in this paper, for which, of course, I alone am responsible: the late Arthur A. Cohen, William Kluback, Richard John Neuhaus, Chaim I. Waxman, and Michael Wyschogrod. —DAVID NOVAK

1. These Jews are advocates of the famous maxim of the early Jewish Enlightenment *(Haskalah)* thinker Judah Leib Gordon (d. 1892), "Be a Jew at home and a human being outside."

relegated it to a very private and esoteric place. Needless to say, this means that they have at most a rather tenuous relationship with Judaism itself, which, in the words of the Talmud, does not approve of "being placed in a corner, only to be studied by whomever wants to do so."[2] And in so restricting the role of religion in their lives, they have, as the studies of Richard John Neuhaus and others make abundantly clear, also departed from the vision of America shared by a large majority of Americans, now or ever.[3] In some significant ways these Jews have become what might be called "constitutional fundamentalists." Like religious fundamentalists (with whom many of these Jews would be horrified to find themselves in the same logical company), they read "sacred texts" (for them, the Constitution of the United States) outside the context of history—either the history of the American people or the history of their own Jewish people. All of this makes their position (at least outside of American courtrooms) rather difficult to advocate. In a significant way, these Jews are among the last doctrinaire secularists in America.[4]

2. Some American Jews see their relationship to America in essentially political terms—that is, they see themselves as members of a special interest group in the overall fabric of American power politics. As a special interest group, Jews have a distinct political agenda of concerns: the military and economic security of the state of Israel, the emigration of Soviet Jews, the elimination of restrictive quotas. Like any successful special interest group in America—and it has been said by friend and foe alike that the Jews might very well be *the* most successful special interest group in America today—Jews have had to argue that their *special* interests in fact coincide with the *general* American interest or, even better, they have argued that they actually promote the general interest. Thus, for example, the valid portrayal of Israel as "the only democracy in the Middle East" not only establishes an affinity between Americans and Israelis but is actually presented as part of the even more forceful argument that Israel is America's only stable and reliable ally in the region.[5]

Usually these Jews are less reluctant to remove their Judaism from their public life. They are more visibly Jewish than most of the previous group. Nevertheless, to a large extent their Jewish self-definition is determined by reaction to external threats: Arab threats to the security of the state of Israel, Soviet threats to Jewish survival in Russia, and the threats of other "minorities" to Jewish opportunity in America. To a certain extent, they confirm the famous thesis of Jean-Paul Sartre that it is anti-

---

2. *Kiddushin* 66a.
3. See *The Naked Public Square* (Grand Rapids: Eerdmans, 1984).
4. See Leo Pfeffer, *Creeds in Competition* (New York: Harper, 1958), pp. 46ff.
5. See Joseph Churba, *The Politics of Defeat: America's Decline in the Middle East* (New York: Cyrco Press, 1977), esp. pp. 166ff.

Semitism which in fact determines who and what is a Jew.[6] Moreover, by being so externally oriented, many of these same Jews have not had sufficient concern for the internal aspects of Jewish survival, what might be called the "cultural" aspects of Jewish life—such matters as Jewish education (especially as intensely pursued in yeshivas and day schools), the threat of intermarriage and cultural assimilation, and the deteriorating Jewish quality of Jewish family life. Not only has this "political" Judaism elevated a part of Judaism (certainly not the most important part) to a level of almost total concern and thus caused more thoughtful and learned Jews to question its ultimate Jewish authenticity, but it also creates problems in dealing with a large segment of Americans—mostly Christian Americans—who do not see political affiliation and activism as the most fundamentally characterizing factor of a community. These Jews are often embarassingly unprepared for what pro-Jewish gentiles now expect from them.

3. Some American Jews see their relationship to America in essentially cultural terms—that is, they see America as a "pluralistic" society in which Jewish cultural identity is to be maintained without a loss of political power or legal rights. For these Jews—and they are certainly not alone in this age of emphasis on ethnicity (most forcefully spearheaded by the whole "black is beautiful" phenomenon)—America is a loose network of ethnic and religious communities having a sort of tacit contract with the polity as a whole—namely, that the various communities will affirm the polity's political and legal primacy in return not merely for the passive tolerance but for the active encouragement of ethnic particularity.[7] Not so long ago, being "American" in the cultural sense entailed behaving like a white Anglo-Saxon Protestant (even if not actually joining the Episcopal Church); now WASPs are no longer role models but just one more ethnic group along with the rest of the immigrants and their children (and not even *primus inter pares*).

This cultural Judaism has led to an even more visible and more internally lived "Jewishness" than that of the "political" Jews. To cite a personal example, I still marvel at the ease my children feel in being practicing Jews in America today compared with the self-consciousness practicing Jews of my generation felt when we were their age (there are also more of "us" now than before).[8]

6. See his *Anti-Semite and Jew*, trans. G. J. Becker (New York: Schocken Books, 1948), pp. 67ff.

7. The great proponent of this idea was Horace M. Kallen; see his *Cultural Pluralism and the American Idea* (Philadelphia: University of Pennsylvania Press, 1956), especially pp. 85ff.

8. See Charles E. Silberman, *A Certain People: American Jews and Their Lives Today* (New York: Summit Books, 1985), pp. 254ff.; and Chaim I. Waxman, *American Jews in Transition* (Philadelphia: Temple University Press, 1983), pp. 124ff.

Nevertheless, one could see this as wanting in terms of the theory of Jewishness more Jews ascribe to than any other (even though fewer actually understand it)—namely, Zionism. For, if the Jews are essentially a cultural group, as Zionism asserts, then their chances for cultural survival and growth are far greater in a society in which they constitute the clear majority, in a land filled with their historical associations, than in a land where they are a small minority of relative newcomers. Jews who place this sort of emphasis on culture are the most vulnerable to the Zionist doctrine of *shelilat ha-golah* ("the negation of the Diaspora"), which asserts that Jewish culture outside of Israel is inevitably doomed, especially when the Jewish state exists and is developing Jewish culture.[9]

Furthermore, although many of these "cultural" Jews would see their culture as inextricable from their religion, their self-definition is rarely based on the classical Jewish doctrines of divine election and covenant. This not only makes their connection with Classical Judaism tenuous but also fails to enable them to respond to the sincere beseeching of those Americans who feel the greatest affinity with the Jewish people (including the state of Israel)—Christians who have cleansed themselves of anti-Semitism, which *they* now regard as anti-Christian. These *friends* look to Jews to speak as the covenanted people of God; they ask for Jews to speak the language of Torah. When Christians asked (often demanded) that we Jews speak in a language *they* assigned us (a language rejecting our own vocabulary from intelligibility), then we were correct to suspect those Jews who were willing to respond in *their* terms. However, this objection hardly applies when we are now being asked by many Christians in America to "instruct us," as Scripture puts it, "from His ways" (Mic. 4:2).

4. Finally, there is a fourth group of Jews, which has always been quite small but which has included some of the most important religious thinkers in the Jewish community, who see their relationship to America in essentially religious terms. Now there is a good deal of overlapping between these "religious" Jews and the "cultural" Jews, especially when "cultural" is not a synonym for "antireligious" as it has been for those who saw *culture* as an almost exclusively linguistic phenomenon (e.g., "Yiddish culture," "Hebrew culture"). Certainly, those whose Judaism is essentially religious are committed to Jewish culture—the Hebrew language, a recognizable and authentic Jewish lifestyle, the state of Isra-

---

9. This doctrine was promulgated at the very beginnings of Zionism. See Ahad Ha-Am's 1909 essay "The Negation of the Diaspora," in *The Zionist Idea: A Historical Analysis and Reader,* ed. A. Hertzberg (Philadelphia: Jewish Publication Society of America, 1959), pp. 270-77. For a critique of this doctrine along cultural lines, see Mordecai M. Kaplan's 1948 essay "The Negation of Jewish Life in the Diaspora" in the same volume, pp. 539-42.

el—for all of these cultural factors have religious origins and structures. (In fact, this could be said about all historical culture. Thus, the error of the antireligious Jewish "culturalists" was based as much on their ignorance or distortion of culture [the term *culture* comes from the Latin *cultus*][10] as it was based on their reduction of Judaism to "Jewishness.")

II

What distinguishes these "religious" Jews from merely "cultural" Jews is their relationship with the non-Jews, which in America primarily means their relationship with Christians. (Although these religious Jews would agree with even the "juridical" Jews and the "political" Jews that we cannot accept the notion of "Christian America," they do recognize to a greater extent than these other types of Jews that Americans are indeed more Christian than anything else.) It is beyond dispute that Classical Judaism in both its scriptural and rabbinic developments has been concerned with what God demands of the gentiles as well as what God demands of the Jews, albeit not equally.[11] Our relationship with American Christians concerns what God demands here and now of our respective communities and how and why these demands do indeed coincide on crucial public issues more often than not.

Heretofore this essentially religious approach to Jewish life in America has taken one of two forms: the first that of Liberal Judaism; the second (and, interestingly enough, the newer phenomenon) that of Traditional Judaism. (I avoid using the denominational labels Orthodox, Conservative, and Reform because they do not apply precisely enough to the intellectual typology I am employing in this essay.)

Liberal Judaism, first in the thought of its German progenitors and later in the thought of their American disciples and successors, in response to the new relationship with the gentiles that came with the Emancipation, developed the idea of the "Mission of Israel." This was the idea that Judaism not only is not a particularistic ethnic "fossil" (to use Toynbee's infamous characterization) to be overcome in the progress of history but that it is the true vanguard of that universal culture which the modern world proclaimed (*Weltgeschichte* in Hegel's terminology)[12] because of its unique theology of "ethical monotheism." The theory of

---

10. See Peter Berger, *The Sacred Canopy* (Garden City, N.Y.: Doubleday, 1969), p. 41.

11. See my *Image of the Non-Jew in Judaism: An Historical and Constructive Study of the Noahide Laws*, Toronto Studies in Theology, vol. 14 (New York: Edwin Mellen Press, 1983), especially chapter 4.

12. See Emil L. Fackenheim, *The Religious Dimension in Hegel's Thought* (Chicago: University of Chicago Press, 1967), pp. 231-33.

ethical monotheism is based on the assumption that the essence of Judaism is its ethical content (which, following Kant, unquestionably the modern philosopher who made the greatest impression on Liberal and even Traditional Jews, is essentially characterized by its *universalizability*).[13] Since this ideal "ethical culture" has not yet been historically realized, and since Judaism and the Jewish people understand and maintain its pristine purity better than all others, Jews are therefore required to preserve their unique cultural and religious identity in the interest of this not-yet-achieved "Messianic" climax of universal history. Those aspects of Jewish tradition that seemed to be not only particularistic but antiuniversal were unworthy of the ethical essence of Judaism and hence stood in need of "reform." In Germany this "reformation" was theorized rather conservatively by such theologians as Hermann Cohen (d. 1918) and Leo Baeck (d. 1956).[14] In America it was more radically theorized and implemented by such theologians as Kaufmann Kohler (d. 1926) and Emil G. Hirsch (d. 1923)[15]—both sons-in-law and disciples of the radical Reform theologian David Einhorn (d. 1879), who had a smaller impact on American Jewish life and thought than they did primarily because he came to America earlier than they, and his speech and writing remained exclusively German.

As the corollary of ethical monotheism or "Prophetic Judaism," the idea of the "Mission of Israel" gained additional impetus in America from arriving at the same time as and possibly from being influenced by the "Social Gospel" school of thought advocated by Walter Rauschenbusch and other Protestant thinkers. All of this was an attempt to see religion as providing the true ethical impetus for a culture and society that were becoming more and more secular in both theory and practice. For Jews especially this was a rather audacious attempt to relate Classical Judaism to contemporary American life without abandoning Judaism altogether as had Rabbi Felix Adler (d. 1933), the founder of the Ethical Culture Movement.[16] One must admire the project as the first real

---

13. See Kant's *Groundwork of the Metaphysic of Morals*, trans. H. J. Paton (New York: Harper & Row, 1964), pp. 88ff.

14. See Cohen, *Religion of Reason out of the Sources of Judaism*, trans. S. Kaplan (New York: Ungar, Frederick, 1972), pp. 283ff.; and Baeck, *The Essence of Judaism*, trans. V. Grubenwieser and L. Pearl (New York: Schocken Books, 1948), pp. 68ff.

15. See Kohler, *Jewish Theology, Systematically and Historically Considered* (1918; rpt., New York: Ktav, 1968), pp. 325ff.; and Hirsch, *My Religion*, ed. G. B. Levi (New York: Macmillan, 1925), pp. 259-62, 288ff.

16. For the sharp reaction to Adler's agnosticism by liberal Jewish thinkers who were most threatened by it, see Benny Kraut, *From Reform Judaism to Ethical Culture: The Religious Evolution of Felix Adler*, Monographs of the Hebrew Union College, no. 5 (Cincinnati: Hebrew Union College Press, 1976), pp. 135ff.

attempt to define a Jewish religious participation in American life exis-
tentially concerned with both Judaism and America as a society in which
Jews need no longer abandon Judaism in order to be true participants.
    Nevertheless, we rarely hear the slogan "Mission of Israel" any
longer, let alone find the idea articulated, even by liberal Jews. I think
this is because it did not find a conceptualization or an expression that
truly spoke to the needs of either the Jews or America.
    First, those liberal Jews who advocated this idea were almost all
anti-Zionists (perhaps the great exception being Stephen S. Wise
[d. 1949]). Zionism, as a nationalistic project for a sovereign Jewish state
in the land of Israel, was anathema to these Jews who saw Judaism's
"mission" as being its ethical teaching and leadership of an essentially
nonsectarian America. However, most Jews (even most Reform Jews
after the 1937 repudiation of the overtly antinationalistic position of
1885) have been too committed to what Mordecai M. Kaplan (d. 1983)
called "Jewish Peoplehood" to define Judaism in what seemed to be
Protestant denominational terms.[17] The Holocaust and the establishment of the state of Israel in the 1940s made this historical persistence an
absolute political necessity. In the end, the Mission of Israel seemed to be
inauthentically Jewish on both cultural-religious and political grounds.
    Second, the social and political program of the advocates of the
Mission of Israel was always rather vague on specific issues. When push
came to shove, they almost always came out in favor of the liberal
political programs of those whose basic outlook was secular. Always in
the background one could hear the ghost of Felix Adler, well-trained
philosopher that he was, cutting away at this theology with Occam's
razor, asking what was uniquely Jewish or should be uniquely Jewish
about this approach (merely to assign its scriptural origins—rather doubtful anyway in its liberalized version—is to commit the congenital fallacy).[18] If it was not, then continuing to call it the Mission *of Israel* could
only smack of chauvinism. One suspects, therefore, that the enthusiasm
for the Mission of Israel expressed from so many pulpits earlier in this
century was more for the sake of showing Judaism to be au courant
intellectually and socially than for the sake of actually attempting to
redirect America in a more Jewishly approved way. Perhaps the greater
ease that third-, fourth-, and even fifth-generation American Jews now

---

17. See Kaplan's *Judaism as a Civilization: Toward a Reconstruction of
American-Jewish Life* (New York: Macmillan, 1934), pp. 227ff. See also the
earlier critique of Ahad Ha-Am in *Selected Essays*, trans. L. Simon (Philadelphia: Jewish Publication Society, 1912), pp. 184ff. Interestingly enough,
Ahad Ha-Am's critique is specifically directed against the version of this idea
proposed by the French traditionalist rabbi S. Munk. The idea was usually, but
not exclusively, proposed by liberal rabbis.
    18. See Kraut, *From Reform Judaism to Ethical Culture*, pp. 169ff.

feel in American culture and society makes these apologetic exercises anachronistic.

However, something akin to the Mission of Israel has emerged in the most unexpected quarters, among some of the most traditional Jewish thinkers in America (though to my knowledge the slogan has never been used by these Jewish thinkers), who are usually characterized by even their fellow Jews as xenophobic in their approach to the general society and culture. To cite a most important example, in 1963, during one of the periods of intense public debate over the perennial issue of prayer in the public schools, Rabbi Moshe Feinstein of New York, without a doubt the most influential halakhic authority among the growing number of American Jews who accept the full authority of the Halakhah—an East European-born and -trained rabbi who to this very day speaks and writes only in Hebrew or Yiddish—was asked about the Jewish approach on this issue. The further irony was that this non-English-speaking (except in private) authority was being asked by a colleague in a community of American Jews where all children are educated in intensely religious parochial schools. (In fact, in this Orthodox milieu, sending one's children to a public primary or secondary school—for some even to a college—would result in instant and severe ostracism.) Why, then, was this question asked and why did Rabbi Feinstein write a pointed response to it, a response widely read by traditional Jews learned enough to understand its content and implications? The answer to this question reveals much about Classical Judaism and the new position of traditional Jews in American culture and society.

Rabbi Feinstein's response draws upon the classical Jewish doctrine of the "Noahide commandments."[19] This doctrine states that whereas the Jews are obligated to observe the 613 commandments in the Pentateuch (along with rabbinic interpretations and additions), the gentiles are obligated to observe the seven commandments the Talmud determined were commanded by God to Adam and Noah and his descendants—that is, to humanity.[20] Two of the foremost commandments are the twin prohibitions of blasphemy and idolatry. Now, based on the logical axiom that the negative presupposes the positive,[21] Rabbi Feinstein quite cogently argued that these prohibitions presuppose an actual relationship with God on the part of the gentiles, the type of relationship that would certainly include regular prayer. Since Judaism by its affirmation of the doctrine of the Noahide commandments obviously approves of this relationship and should therefore advocate it, Rabbi Feinstein concluded that Normative Judaism can express approval of prayer in the public schools.

---

19. *Igrot Mosheh: Orah Hayyim* (New York, 1963), 2:196-98, no. 25.
20. See my *Image of the Non-Jew in Judaism.*
21. See *Nedarim* 11b.

Rabbi Feinstein's response indicates that, contrary to popular prejudice, traditional Jews are in fact concerned with the moral and spiritual life of the general society at large (although he is not entirely comfortable with taking a public stand on this issue). It is only that this has not been a concern to which the tradition assigns top priority in comparison with more internal Jewish concerns. The raison d'être of Judaism is not to teach the gentiles but to obey God's Torah, whether the gentiles are interested in it or not. (The theological weakness of the liberal Mission of Israel idea was that it seemed to be a good deal more interested in the approval of the gentiles than in the approval of God.) If, however, the gentiles do see light in Israel (Isa. 42:6), then, as an ancient rabbinic text puts it, they should "send their representatives and take the Torah for themselves."[22] Nevertheless, Rabbi Feinstein's seriousness in dealing with this topic at all indicates two important sociological facts: (1) traditional Jews are now enough a part of American culture and society that they must have an opinion on such questions of public debate, and (2) traditional Jews are concerned that America develop along ethical and religious lines that are not antithetical to Judaism's *theocratic* worldview[23]—namely, that the revealed Law of God is to be the basic norm for every society and for every human person. This is for the sake of the survival of both Judaism and civilization itself.

For both existential and intellectual reasons I am in basic sympathy with this approach, which is certainly in the spirit of Classical Judaism (i.e., the Judaism formulated in Scripture and rabbinic literature). But it has to be developed further in order that it might speak more directly to the great crisis of values we are now living through in American democracy.

The problem with this approach, at least as heretofore articulated by its traditionalist spokesmen, is that it is "theocratic," which is to say that it deduces legal prescriptions from religious texts, something that seems to run counter to the tendency of our democracy from the founding fathers until the present. Indeed, Maimonides, one of the greatest formulators of Classical Judaism, spoke about *forcing* the gentiles to follow the Noahide commandments—if Jews, of course, have the power to do so.[24] This difficulty with applying theocratic norms in a democracy that if not secularist is certainly nonsectarian has also been faced by Roman Catholic traditionalists. And, indeed, we traditional Jews can

---

22. *Tosefta Sotah* 8:6. For the ancient rabbinic recognition of the universal human need for both laudatory and petitionary prayer, see *Berakhot* 20b; *Sotah* 10a-b; 35b.

23. Judaism was first characterized as a "theocracy" by Josephus (see *Contra Apionem*, 2.164-67).

24. *Mishneh Torah: Hilkhot Melakhim*, 8.10. See my *Image of the Non-Jew in Judaism*, pp. 53-56.

learn much from someone like the Jesuit theologian John Courtney Murray, who made such strides in keeping Roman Catholic ethical teaching from being rejected by Americans as ipso facto theocratic and hence "un-American."[25]

III

Many assume that there is a dichotomy between religious doctrine and democracy that is insuperable in our society, but I would like to assert that a closer look at how theology functions in the history of Judaism and how religious doctrine functions in the history of America might well show that there is no such dichotomy.

Let me begin with two personal recollections, the type of oral reports of the words of teachers in which the discourse of the Talmud abounds.

In the autumn of 1957 I entered the undergraduate college of the University of Chicago. One of the courses I was required to take that first year was Social Sciences I, which dealt with the history of American political thought. At the same time, I was already intensely involved in the study of the Talmud, particularly in a tractate *(Baba Kama)* that deals with Jewish civil law. It was the custom at that time for distinguished professors in fields relating to our course of study to be invited to lecture to the combined sections of the course periodically. Two of these lectures made a lasting impression on my thinking and I still remember them quite well.

In the first lecture, William Thomas Hutchinson (d. 1976), an expert on American constitutional history, presented the thesis that the reason the American Constitution of 1789 was far more enduring than the constitution promulgated in France shortly thereafter is that the former was the result of almost two hundred years of colonial experience, whereas the latter was the result of purely philosophical speculation. What Hutchinson was presenting, it seems in retrospect, was a common law view of American history, contending that theory is enunciated only after sufficient precedent has been accumulated for a deliberate judgment to be made.[26]

---

25. See *We Hold These Truths* (Garden City, N.Y.: Doubleday, 1960), especially chapter 5. For ancient Jewish suspicions of the combination of ecclesiastical and royal power, see *Kiddushin* 66a and *Yerushalmi: Horayot* 3.2/47c.

26. Along these lines, consider the following exchange from Robert Bolt's A *Man For All Seasons:*

ROPER: Then you set man's law above God's!

MORE: No, far below; but let *me* draw your attention to a fact—I'm *not* God.

The second lecture I remember that year was by Avery Craven (d. 1980), a historian whose specialty was the period around the Civil War. Craven presented the thesis that the real preamble to the Constitution of the United States was not what is formally called the "preamble" but rather the Declaration of Independence. He illustrated his point by analyzing the institution of slavery. On strictly constitutional grounds, slavery was permitted and slaves had the status of chattel. That point was made with legal cogency by Chief Justice Roger B. Taney in the famous Dred Scott decision of 1857. However, the Declaration of Independence, despite the fact that it was written by Virginia slaveholder Thomas Jefferson, declared that "all men are created equal" (a theological statement if there ever was one, despite the fact that it was made by the nonchurchgoing Deist Jefferson). According to Craven, the Civil War and the resulting thirteenth amendment to the Constitution outlawing slavery affirmed the priority of the philosophical foundation of the Constitution over specific legal reasoning in a matter of crucial importance in the life of this democracy. In fact, as I recall, Craven went so far as to say that had the events that made the thirteenth amendment possible not taken place, it is doubtful whether our constitutional form of government would have endured.[27]

Now, on the surface, the theses of Hutchinson and Craven seem to contradict one another. Hutchinson emphasized the priority of precedent over theory, whereas Craven emphasized the priority of theory over precedent. However, upon deeper examination they are in truth complementary in the sense that they both draw on a dialectic between precedent and theory. Precedent by definition is historically prior, but precedent does lead to theory, which then begins to serve as a guide specifying which precedents ought subsequently to be emphasized and which ought to be deemphasized. Once there is enough precedent behind a theory, that theory becomes regulative, a *conditio sine qua non* for the further development of the *system* of precedent. When precedents are invoked that ignore the tendency of the system's development, then theory must *inform* the process of selection. It functions as a criterion of judgment. The relation is dialectical in that neither the theoretical pole nor the practical pole can be reduced to the other. Thus, the theory is more than an inductive generalization from the precedents, and the

---

The currents and eddies of right and wrong, which you find such plain sailing, I can't navigate. I'm no voyager. . . . This country's planted thick with laws from coast to coast—man's laws, not God's—and if you cut them down . . . d'you think you could stand upright in the winds that would blow then?

27. See Craven's *Civil War in the Making* (Baton Rouge: Louisiana State University Press, 1959), pp. 64ff.; see also Carl Becker, *The Declaration of Independence* (New York: Harcourt Brace, 1922), p. 6.

precedents are not simply deduced from the theory. Like an electrical current, the full socio-political reality lies between the two poles.

Even in those earlier days of my education, it seemed to me that something similar was also taking place in Normative Judaism. Later on, when I began to write about Jewish thought, I systematically examined the relation of theology and law in Jewish tradition.[28] Now in Normative Judaism ethics is law, and the ethical-legal structure is theological in the sense that its origin is seen in God's will and its purpose is seen as being the highest good—that being the nearness of God (Ps. 73:28). Any attempt, therefore, to remove Jewish ethics from its overall theological context is ultimately incredible. However, this does not mean that law *(halakhah)* is deduced from theology *(aggadah)*. The law in its immediate manifestation has a life of its own, developing along lines of precedent and the human assessment of human situations; as the Talmud puts it, "the human judge can only judge what his human eyes see."[29] This is important because it enables the law to draw upon a wealth of human experience and it encourages creative human judgment to operate. This mitigates, to a great extent, the type of dogmatism that attempts to force all experience and judgment quickly into a procrustean bed, the type of dogmatism that too readily has the answer before the question itself has been adequately experienced and formulated.[30]

Nevertheless, in the great issues that the law has faced—issues dealing with fundamental questions of the essence of human personhood, the sanctity of human sexuality, the nature of human sociality, the vocation of the Jewish people—in these great issues the system of precedent is insufficient in and of itself because it is usually ambiguous, presenting prima facie conflicting options for judgment. It is ambiguous precisely because the authorities of the past could not solve all problems in advance; they could not be substitutes for the living authorities of the present and the future.[31]

At these crucial points, the great authorities invoked the theological principles developed on the nonlegal side of Classical Judaism. But, let it be emphasized, they invoked these principles when and only when there was at least some purely legal precedent for them to choose.

---

28. See my *Law and Theology in Judaism* (New York: Ktav, 1974-76), 1:1ff. and 2:xiiiff.; and *Halakhah in a Theological Dimension* (Chico, Cal.: Scholars Press, 1985), pp. 11ff., 61ff.

29. *Sanhedrin* 6b. Although the Law is *from Heaven* (*Mishnah: Sanhedrin* 10.1) and is *for the sake of Heaven* (*Mishnah: Abot* 2:12), it is, nevertheless, not *in Heaven* (*Baba Metzia* 59b on Deut. 30:12).

30. This seems to be the meaning of the rabbinic maxim "Be deliberate in judgment" (*Mishnah: Abot* 1.1; see Maimonides' comment thereon).

31. See *Rosh Hashanah* 25a-b on Deut. 17:9 and *Menahot* 29b.

When the great issues (what contemporary legal theorists call "hard cases") arose, the system of precedent was indeed not sufficient in and of itself, but it was nonetheless still necessary. Thus, for example, when the whole theology of Kabbalah began to be fully explicated in the late Middle Ages, there was a tendency in some circles to see its main document, the *Zohar*, as having achieved a normative status equal to and even surpassing the Talmud. On the other hand, there were those authorities who regarded it as antinomian and therefore having no normative status at all. Finally, in the early sixteenth century, the Egyptian authority Rabbi David ibn Abi Zimra ruled that in and of itself the law of the Talmud takes normative precedence over the theology of the *Zohar*. However, when the law of the Talmud is itself ambiguous (as it frequently and thankfully is), presenting conflicting precedents and opinions, then the theology of the *Zohar* may be invoked as a criterion of judgment, emphasizing one tendency and deemphasizing (but never totally eliminating) the other.[32]

IV

The application of all of this to the crisis of values in America today can be the new agenda of the Mission of Israel, an agenda far more authentically Jewish and socially critical than that of the earlier liberal proponents of this idea.

The crisis of values in America today has become evident in the great issues of social debate that have emerged during the past three decades, issues that have inevitably been involved in landmark legal decisions.

Let us take the most persistent and intense issue of social debate in America for over a decade—abortion—an issue that shows no signs whatsoever of being any less controversial during the next decade. It is the focus of so much attention because it deals with the most fundamental moral issue possible, the definition of human personhood and society's role in relation to it. Because it is patently clear that this sort of moral question cannot be reduced to merely legal precedent, the 1973 *Roe vs. Wade* decision of the U.S. Supreme Court by no means settled the issue; if anything, it exacerbated it. Here we have a clear conflict of values, a *Kulturkampf* with monumental ramifications.

---

32. See *Responsa Rodbaz* (Warsaw: n.p., 1882), no. 1,111; and Louis Jacobs, *Theology in the Responsa* (London: Routledge & Kegan Paul, 1975), pp. 122-23. For contemporary philosophical emphasis of creative judgment over and above "objective" description, see, for example, M. Polanyi, *The Study of Man* (Chicago, 1959), pp. 12-13.

The legal system is ambiguous enough to call for extralegal factors in making a judgment. The fourteenth amendment to the Constitution speaks of the right of every "person" to "equal protection of the laws." However, nowhere does it define personhood. As such, a human fetus, whose personhood is by no means immediately evident, may or may not be entitled to the *equal* protection the Constitution mandates for *persons* and only persons. Here is where the legal system must look at systems of value to supply such definitions. And, here is where we see in bold relief the clash of values. For, if the fetus has the status of a person, in that it is the result of the creative sexual act of two human persons (unambiguously and irreducibly human persons, not things, because of their status as *imago Dei*), then it is subject to the same protection of the law as his or her parents.[33] If, on the other hand, personhood is determined by such other criteria as viability, independence, speech, rationality, quality of life, or whatever, then a very different interpretation of the Constitution inevitably follows.

Now, even adopting the first theologically grounded view does not automatically solve the subsequent legal questions, as some pro-life advocates naively think.[34] Accepting this broadest definition of human personhood does not solve questions of mortal conflict *between* persons, for example, such as the question of whether the fetus can in some cases be regarded as an unwarranted intruder (*rodef*) in the womb of another person—as in cases of rape. These questions have been intensely debated in Jewish tradition, and there is considerable literature on the subject even in English.[35] It has generally been assumed that no one in the Normative (i.e., *halakhic*) tradition of Judaism can cogently assign the fetus the status of nonperson on the level of a thing, having no rights at all. Conversely, no one can cogently maintain that the life of the fetus takes precedence over that of his or her mother. The real question—involving the hard cases—is how widely or narrowly we are to interpret situations of "threatening intrusion."

In the context of Jewish tradition no one can simply say, "based on my theological principles, this is the only ethical course of action." When legal precedent already exists, one can use his or her theological principles only to exercise judgment and persuade others. This is also the case in the American tradition. Those who say that religion may not determine the law in our constitutional democracy, that religion may not

---

33. See my *Law and Theology in Judaism*, 1:114ff.
34. See Germain Grisez, *Abortion: The Myths, the Realities, the Arguments* (New York: Corpus Books, 1970), esp. pp. 267ff.
35. See, for example, D. M. Feldman, *Birth Control in Jewish Law* (New York: New York University Press, 1968), pp. 251ff.; and J. D. Bleich, *Contemporary Halakhic Problems* (New York: Ktav, 1977), pp. 325ff.

impose its values on the society as a whole, are technically correct. The Constitution not only protects us from being subject to the rule of any religious community but even protects the nonreligious minority (and let it be emphasized that they are the *minority*) from being subject to the rule of a consensus of all or most of the religious communities (a rather hypothetical state of affairs at present and in the foreseeable future). However, it is totally unwarranted to infer from this social fact that the absence of religion from the process of *specific* legal reasoning requires its elimination from the *general* realm of social discourse and persuasion (as opposed to political coercion). Such an inference is a case of the fallacy of generalization. For, if this inference is made, then we are indeed left with what Richard John Neuhaus calls "the naked public square."[36] If "naked" is synonymous with "vacuous," then history as well as nature (to paraphrase Aristotle) abhors a vacuum, and the vacuum is inevitably filled with the type of secularism that makes the elimination of religion from the society qua society its own dogma.

It seems to me that the intention of our American doctrine of the separation of church and state is to deny the legitimacy of deducing politically acceptable action from dogma—anyone's dogma. But aside from that type of dogmatic deduction (so obvious among those who engage in one-issue politics), one's dogmas and doctrines should be brought into the public square, especially when it can be shown that they have strong affinities with the dogmas and doctrines that *inspired* American democracy in the first place and that sustained it at times of great crisis in its history.

The point made so tellingly by the late German-American Protestant theologian Paul Tillich, that no one really acts without an "ultimate concern," is especially germane.[37] For it means that no area of human discourse and action is value-free, and it is better for the operation of

---

36. Charles E. Silberman in his widely discussed book, *A Certain People*, criticizes Neuhaus—inaccurately and unfairly, I think—for advocating "an explicitly Christian society" (p. 357). Yet, read in context, Neuhaus (*The Naked Public Square*, pp. 80ff.) is *describing* the true state of affairs about the values of most Americans. He is not prescribing a "Christian America," which would exclude Jews and other Americans whose values come from non-Christian sources. See further *The Naked Public Square*, p. 127, and note the following on p. 261: "For a revival of religion to help in leading us out of the dark night of cultural contradictions there must be a profound security about the relationship between Christians and Jews . . . we must ponder anew the divine mystery of living Judaism. . . . For good reasons, Jews and others who are uneasy about the idea of 'Christian America' will continue to prefer the naked square until it is manifest that Christians have internalized—as a matter of doctrine, even of dogma—reverence for democratic dissent."

37. See Tillich's *Dynamics of Faith* (New York: Harper, 1957), pp. 1ff.

one's values to be publicly visible and thus socially responsible and responsive than to keep one's values a purely private matter and thus run the risk of becoming socially irresponsible and unresponsive (i.e., "dogmatic" in the pejorative sense of that term). Here too the late American Protestant theologian Reinhold Niebuhr still has much to teach all of us about how biblical theism can be seen as the most adequate foundation for democracy without making it "theocratic" (which literally means "the rule of God," but usually means "the rule of church").[38]

V

The concluding question to be addressed is one my grandfather used to ask: "So, is all of this good or bad for the Jews?"

Well, I believe that this is good for the Jews—very good—because I believe that Judaism has some very important points to make in the moral and legal discourse of our society. There is a Mission of Israel, and the exercise of that "missionary" project is totally consistent with the cultural, political, even juridical interests of Jews in American society.

First, if we Jews regard ourselves as having a mission in America today, then we obviously cannot accept the Zionist doctrine of the "negation of the diaspora" *(shelilat ha-golah)*. This does not mean, however, that we can or should return to the anti-Zionism of the earlier liberal Jewish proponents of this idea. We Jews are a community constituted by the Torah,[39] and that alone makes us quite different from a "denomina-

38. For a still astute appreciation of Niebuhr on this point, see Arthur Schlesinger, Jr., "Reinhold Niebuhr's Role in American Political Thought and Life," in *Reinhold Niebuhr: His Religious, Social, and Political Thought*, ed. C. W. Kegley and R. W. Bretall (New York: Macmillan, 1956), pp. 126ff. And note T. S. Eliot's statement that "The term 'democracy' as I have said again and again, does not contain enough positive content to stand alone against the forces that you dislike—it can easily be transformed by them. If you will not have God (and He is a jealous God), you should pay your respects to Hitler or Stalin" (*The Idea of a Christian Society*, 2nd ed. [London: Faber & Faber, 1982], p. 82). It might seem odd that I would quote, of all people, T. S. Eliot, who it is assumed was an anti-Semite. That he was is incontrovertible—that is, before his conversion to Anglican Christianity in 1927. After that, he underwent a moral conversion as well. One should read, for example, his moving appeal on behalf of the Jews of France in 1941 (*The Idea of a Christian Society*, p. 138).

39. As the ninth-century Jewish theologian Rabbi Saadyah Gaon put it, "our nation of the children of Israel is only a nation by virtue of its laws" (*The Book of Beliefs and Opinions*, trans. S. Rosenblatt, Yale Judaica Series, vol. 1 [New Haven: Yale University Press, 1948], p. 158).

tion" in the American Protestant sense of that term. Our Torah-con-
stituted community must be concerned with the land and state of Israel,
nonobservant—even atheistic—Jews, the Hebrew language, and other
"ethnic" matters. (The Greek *ethnos* means "people," and the Torah
certainly designates us as a people; because of that designation as A*m
Yisrael*—"the people who strive with God" [Gen. 32:29]—I resist any
secularist interpretation of Jewish "peoplehood.") The fact that we affirm
that the Lord God of Israel is also Creator of heaven and earth, and the
fact that we are bound by the law and teaching of the Torah *wherever* we
happen to live, indicates on religious grounds the validity of any Jewish
community to exist anywhere the Torah can be studied and the commandments observed.[40] Furthermore, we are morally bound to support
in every way a society that allows us the freedom to live as authentic Jews
and that itself is bound by a law we consider grounded in the law of God
for all humankind. None of this implies that American Jews denigrate or
even bracket in any way the unique Jewish status of the land and state of
Israel. It simply means that we American Jews can cogently argue on
precise Jewish religious grounds that America has value for us and that we
have value for America. I emphasize this because I believe that the
religious and intellectual life of American Jewry has been impoverished
by the assumption—consciously maintained by some, unconsciously by
others—that Jewish life in America is at best transient, that America is a
trayfe medinah (literally, "a nonkosher society," a charge made at the
turn of this century by some East European rabbis who attempted to
dissuade—mostly unsuccessfully—their flocks from joining the mass
migration to America), that Jewish life in America is ultimately impossi-
ble. There is little in Jewish tradition and little in American Jewish
experience (as recent studies have now shown)[41] to validate this view.
(Hopefully, it will become a topic of more and more dialogue between
Israeli and American Jews.)

Second, there are values about which Judaism and American Jews
can profitably *inform* American social and political life. Since Jews and
Judaism have suffered so, especially in this century of incomparable
horrors, perhaps it is best to express them as a series of negations or
prophetic warnings.

1. Judaism and American Jews have a good deal to warn America
about concerning the danger of depersonalization in our society. The
most valuable aspect for society of the Jewish doctrine of the human
person as the image of God is that it gives the widest definition of human

---

40. See *Mishnah Kiddushin* 1.9 and *Kiddushin* 37a.
41. See note 8 herein.

personhood possible without eliminating the equally important distinction between the human and the nonhuman.[42] The tendency in the twentieth century has been the exact opposite—namely, to limit personhood based on arbitrary factors such as physical condition, race, age, and so on. This has been done by the state in the person of those who have the political power to do so. Here is where Judaism and the experience of the Jews once again coalesce: the Jews have been the most agonized victims of the denial of this doctrine of Judaism. Those Jews who are intent that Americans (let alone Europeans, who were closer to the scene of the crime) "never forget" the Holocaust and all that led up to it and made it possible must eschew arbitrary definitions of human personhood so contrary to both Torah and Jewish experience.

2. Judaism and American Jews have a good deal to warn America about concerning the danger of deculturization in our society. Not only does Judaism encourage Jews to live according to our own traditions and culture but it also encourages non-Jews to do the same. This can best be illustrated by a hasidic story my late revered teacher Rabbi Abraham Joshua Heschel once told me about Rabbi Israel Baal Shem Tov, the founder of the hasidic movement in eighteenth-century Poland. It seems that the Baal Shem Tov had a Catholic coachman. One day when out riding, they passed the shrine of a saint, the type that dotted the Polish countryside. The coachman did not make the sign of the cross when they passed by it. The Baal Shem Tov immediately ordered his close disciple who was with him then to fire the man. He reasoned that if his own was no longer sacred for him, he certainly would not respect what was sacred for someone else. The story is typical of very sound and persistent Jewish doctrine.[43]

The modern industrial process of deculturization, turning everyone into a similar copy of his or her neighbor, thereby imitating the mass production of our own machines, creates a dangerous cultural and emotional vacuum. It denies an overall purpose to human life and simultaneously destroys our link with the past that once did reveal such purposes to us.[44] As such, it makes modern societies vulnerable to the likes of Hitler, whose simplistic appeals to fears and fantasies no longer had to face, in any strong sense, the mediating safeguards of subtle and multifaceted tradition. Those Jews who delight in being in the foreground of all that is irreverently avante-garde should ponder whether similar Jewish contributions to the traditionless culture of Weimar Germany may not have destroyed those aspects of German historical culture

---

42. See my *Halakhah in a Theological Dimension*, pp. 96ff.
43. See my *Image of the Non-Jew in Judaism*, pp. 130ff.
44. See my *Rise of the Unmeltable Ethnics* (New York: Macmillan, 1973), especially pp. xxxiiiff.

that might have served as better bases of resistance to Hitler had they not been so discredited already.[45] Here again, we see how Torah enlightens Jewish experience and how Jewish experience illustrates Torah.

3. Judaism and American Jews can also teach America about the dialectic between faith and history. The problem with so much of Christian moral teaching in America, especially *traditional* Christian moral teaching (Catholic, orthodox, evangelical), is its fundamentalism. Now *fundamentalism* means many things, but it seems to be characterized by a conviction that "all the answers are right here in the Book," and that it is only obstinacy or ignorance that prevents God's plan from being implemented and immediately healing all our social ills. (In this sense, "fundamentalism" is certainly not an essentially Christian outlook; much of the traditionalist Jewish community is just as fundamentalistic.) According to this view, history, the accumulated experience of highly fallible humans, has no value; indeed, it constitutes a threat to the Truth. Here is where the Jewish obsession with the *Law*—so often denigrated by Christians who misread Paul—is germane.[46] For, as we have seen, the Law is not a divine oracle that lights up whenever we approach it with a question. The Law is, rather, a historically developing system that subjects the most cogently argued theory to the collective precedents of the centuries-old community. Fundamentalism is impatient with this slow, often bumbling process, and this is precisely why, in our century especially, it has been so easily manipulated by all sorts of political fanatics who offer instant solutions to complex social problems. The Law saves us from this type of utopian pseudo-messianism, just as it saves us from the relativistic vacuum wherein all norms are taken simply as matters of taste and therefore outside the range of rational discourse.[47]

For these reasons I believe that America today provides a unique religious challenge to Judaism and the American Jews. It seems that at long last we are being taken seriously by some of the most thoughtful elements in American society, and we are being taken seriously as "Jewish Jews." How seriously we will take ourselves will depend largely on the Jewish piety, learning, and insight of those whom we make the leaders of

---

45. On this, see chapter 2 of George L. Mosse's *German Jews beyond Judaism* (Bloomington, Ind.: Indiana State University Press, 1985).

46. See W. D. Davies, *Paul and Rabbinic Judaism*, 2d ed. (London: S.P.C.K., 1955), pp. 69ff.

47. Solomon Goldman asks, "What brought pauper and prince, foolish and wise, poor and rich, slave and master together? What was the magic spell that chased away all distinction? It was the Law. Nobody could live outside it or above it. . . . It was the Law that spared to Judaism the gruesome inhumanities of religious madness" (*The Jew and the Universe* [New York: Harper, 1936], p. 179).

our community in America. Heretofore we American Jews, contrary to the tendency of almost all of previous Jewish history, have hardly looked for piety, learning, or Jewish insight in our leaders. But the times have changed radically. We must be up to them, demanding that those who speak about us and for us be capable, spiritually and intellectually, to articulate and implement our unique destiny in America.[48]

---

48. Arthur A. Cohen states that "What is required now is the critique of culture in the light of Jewish teaching . . . [to] offer the Jewish community periodic reports that would document the assertion of the tradition (its 'supernatural' dimension) regarding the immediate social and political concerns the Jewish community faces" ("Embarrassed by Principle," *Present Tense* 12 [Winter 1985]: 41).

The Story of an Encounter

by Paul T. Stallsworth

On January 23 and 24, 1985, a conference of scholars that was convened by the Rockford Institute Center on Religion and Society explored the notion that, contrary to conventional wisdom, America is not a secular society. Indeed, by the end of this conference, entitled "Unsecular America," it was agreed that American society is a singularly religious society and that religion in American public life is increasing in visibility and influence. Much of this publicly resurgent religion, of course, is of Christian, and specifically Protestant, orientation. So it was fitting and proper to have discussed these matters in the rather WASPish surroundings of the Princeton Club of New York.

Quite naturally, a very important question arises: How does and how might the American Jewish community perceive and respond to this most recent eruption of religion in American public life? To address that and many related questions, the Center on Religion and Society joined Temple Emanu-El of New York City to sponsor the conference "Jews in Unsecular America," nearly one year after the "Unsecular America" conference. For two days—January 13 and 14, 1986—eighteen scholars gathered around a conference table in the boardroom of the Temple to mull over the issues pertaining to Jews and Judaism in American public life. A report on the table talk of "Jews in Unsecular America" follows.

Large portraits of the distinguished and learned rabbis who have served Temple Emanu-El through the generations line the walls of the board room. In the midst of the silent presence of his predecessors, Ronald B. Sobel, the current senior rabbi at the Temple and cohost of the con-

ference, broke the ice with his introductory remarks. He placed two
Jewish communities, one local and the other national, in their historical
contexts.

"Prior to the American Jewish experience," he said, "it is highly
unlikely that any Jewish community anywhere would have had a major
synagogue on the major avenue of the greatest city in the nation. And the
fact that the American Jewish community was able to erect on *the* avenue
in *the* city this kind of a synagogue [Temple Emanu-El on Fifth Avenue],
I think, is rather reflective of what the American Jewish community was
able to become. This thing that we call the American Jewish community
was given its shape and its character by the Emancipation and the Enlightenment, two events that are certainly closely related but that the
American Jew really does not have any first-hand experience with. When
we speak of the emergence of the American Jew with the American
Jewish community, we are really speaking about waves of immigration.
But nevertheless, there were certain assumptions implicit in the Emancipation and the Enlightenment that became very dominant factors in
shaping the American Jew, and part of it was a liberal consensus. Well
that liberal consensus has undergone some major trauma, certainly in
the last twenty years."

If the notion of a "liberal consensus" in the American Jewish
community is commonly accepted by those who think about such things,
the notion of a traumatized liberal consensus is not. Commenting on this
and other matters from his view at an office of the American Jewish
Committee, Milton Himmelfarb presented the first paper of the
conference.

PUBLIC JUDAISM TODAY

Himmelfarb started the conferees' examination of the contemporary Jewish community's stance toward and position in the public arena of
American life. His remarks and the remarks that they generated covered
Jewish opinion on church-state issues, recent Jewish assertiveness in
public, meanings of anti-Semitism, the religious knowledge of Jews, and
the new "unsecular" climate in America today.

Jews, Church, and State

Himmelfarb contended that Jewish opinion on church-state questions—
tuition tax credits, prayer in public schools, and the like—points in the
separationist direction. But what is most surprising about this opinion is
the degree to which Jewish leadership agrees with the rank and file on

these questions, because leadership groups usually tend to wander away ideologically from their constituencies.

"Spokesmen for groups do not necessarily represent the actual opinion of most members of the groups," said Himmelfarb. "Stanley Rothman and his protégés the Lichters have shown that the spokesmen for black Americans do not have the same opinions as the mass of black Americans. In Protestantism it is notorious that the bureaucracies of the various churches are far to the left of the people who sit in the pews. That does not work in the American Jewish community. With respect to church-state issues, positions taken by the major institutions of the Jewish community—whether it is the Union of American-Hebrew Congregations or the American Jewish Committee or the Anti-Defamation League or the American Jewish Congress or so on down the line—do indeed reflect the opinions of most Jews in the United States. I would go further to say not just the opinions but the deep convictions, the instincts, the strong beliefs. I am able to say that with a fair degree of confidence because in the past few years at the American Jewish Committee we have sponsored opinion polls of American Jews and are reasonably satisfied that the people who answered the questions in those polls are representative of American Jews."

Given the Jewish community's solidly separationist sentiments, one can easily understand its almost knee-jerk resistance to questioning or undermining what has been called by Richard John Neuhaus "the naked public square." Himmelfarb argued that most American Jews wanted and want the American public square to remain relatively free of religious reference, and he explained why by way of a brief lesson in history and historical memory.

"Earlier in American history there was an imposition of a kind of nonsectarian, pan-Protestantism in the public school system," said Himmelfarb, "complete with reciting the Lord's Prayer every morning. There are memories about that. [Michael Novak will recount some in the text following.] Of the two alternatives that Jonathan Sarna describes so well—a kind of plural establishment where all religions are equal and equally well regarded and de facto favored, and total separationism—most Jews hold to the total separationism and reject plural establishment. There are compromises around the edges—for example, the Hanukkah menorah in Central Park. Many Jews do not like it. It is too much of a concession to an inroad, too much of a breach in that wall of separation, which is a favorite metaphor of Jews. It is fair to say that the large majority of American Jews is on the total separationist side, rather than on the plural establishment side."

For decades the Jewish community's total separationist convictions were unknown to the greater society. Himmelfarb picked up the historical lesson where he had left off.

"Until about forty years ago Jews, as a matter of prudence, kept a very low profile. While Jews deeply resented the Lord's Prayer in the schools, we knew better than to make a public fuss over it. Then there was an annual Christmas crisis all over the United States. By the way, you can write that news story right now, withhold specific names, and use the same story year after year. Forty years ago the same practices went on only more so, except that Jews were not brave enough—or imprudent enough—to protest against it because the cost of protest would have been too high."

All of a sudden in the 1940s the American Jewish community came out of hiding. It—or at least segments of it—entered the public square in a new and rather assertive way. Several conference participants proposed possible reasons for this public entry. Himmelfarb traced Jewish assertiveness to socio-economic factors.

"Precisely as the condition and status of Jews in the United States improved and as the self-confidence of American Jews grew stronger, their protest against Protestant culture began and strengthened."

Quite unexpectedly, Stanley Rothman of the Department of Government at Smith College, expressed Himmelfarb's point by raising the flag of "oppression."

"When restrictions break down, people begin to see new options. In many cases, when reform is underway, more options are seen by those who consider themselves oppressed in some way. It is not a question of prudence. Before reform begins, people just do not see possibilities which they later come to see."

Accepting these sociological explanations of Jewish assertiveness in the 1940s, Jonathan Sarna of the Hebrew Union College–Jewish Institute of Religion and the Center for the Study of the American Jewish Experience added to them. He tied the Jewish community's increasingly public role to its strategy of taking its battle to the courts. "Jewish assertiveness arose largely in the post–World War II era in part because there began to be tests in the courts and eventually in the U.S. Supreme Court. There simply were not any challenges under freedom of religion and the First Amendment until that period. For almost a century nobody brought up such cases. But then there was a series of decisions that was situated within the Jewish community and that began to be debated nationwide. Because church-state policy began to be articulated by the Supreme Court, what had been an internal issue in the Jewish community became an external issue."

At this point in the conference discussion, Marvin Wilson of Gordon College raised a significant question: Did the Holocaust during World War II and the establishment of the state of Israel in 1948 contribute to Jewish assertiveness in America? Himmelfarb cautiously doubted the link for intuitive reasons.

"I doubt it personally, but I have no great proof. I think Holocaust is something that people like us talk about while sitting around this kind of table and while having this kind of discussion. But I do not think that for non-Jewish men and women in the street in the United States Holocaust has ever been of any significance. We did a recent poll in which we found that many Americans just wish that Jews would stop talking about Holocaust. Enough already! Call for a forty-year statute of limitations, or whatever you want to call it, on the subject. That is why I am doubtful about the Holocaust proposition. And I do not see any direct connection with Israel. At most it would be indirect and by way of psychology. It would not be a socially or politically direct connection."

Not so fast, urged Charles Silberman, author of the widely noted book on the current state of American Jews, *A Certain People*. He suggested that the American public's knowledge of the Holocaust helped to diminish anti-Semitism in American life and that, in turn, the less anti-Semitic culture was much more receptive to the Jewish community's public position.

"There was an extraordinary drop in anti-Semitism immediately after World War II. This cannot be explained on any basis other than the impact of the awareness of the Holocaust on American opinion. This decline has no precedent in the history of public opinion polling."

Silberman added another possible explanation for the rise of American Jewish presence in public—the advent of the naked public square.

"The transformation in the position of Jews in American society—the new confident sense of being part of the mainstream, of being perceived as Americans rather than the eternal other or the stranger—is closely correlated if not necessarily caused by the removal of clothing from the public square. As the United States moved from being a clearly Protestant society with a Catholic minority and with Jews as outsiders into a pluralistic society with no established religion, the position of Jews changed. One cannot understand the visceral attachment to separationism apart from that correlation."

The American Jewish community, with all of its separationist agenda, said Silberman, made its presence known most fully when the greater culture began leaning in the separationist direction. Thus the Jewish community simply reinforced what was already occurring in American public life.

As if it is not enough to be a congregational rabbi and a profesor of philosophy at the City University of New York and now at the Jewish Theological Seminary of America, David Novak briefly assumed the psychoanalyst's role. He tried to describe why some Jews were so assertive in stripping bare the public square.

"With a few exceptions those Jews who have been in the forefront of de-Christianizing America were people of minimal Jewish commitment, minimal Jewish knowledge, who, I am convinced, in their heart of hearts were really threatened by the fact that a Christian America requires that Jews be more Jewish. It is expected of them. Whereas in a secularized America, one does not have to be more Jewish. It is the classic psychoanalytic notion of projection. Basically such antireligiousness is often against Judaism. It is Judaism that is gotten rid of. It is Judaism that is suppressed. But this is projected on the majority culture. The real Jewish fascination with secularism as a doctrine in and of itself is precisely that it offers a way out of Judaism. That is something that has to be discussed within the Jewish community. Anti-Judaic and, I am not just talking about Jews, self-hating people who were afraid of their Jewish names and changed them have always been in the forefront of secularizing America."

Friends of the Community

Whatever the reason or reasons the Jewish community went public, it is at least beyond dispute that it did go public. A point of interest, then, is who this community newly entered into the American mainstream perceived to be its friends and enemies. Himmelfarb began discussion of this point by answering the question in mainly political, left-right terms.

"American Jews have certain perceptions about who their friends are and who their enemies are. These perceptions are not very firmly based in reality. They are, however, based on a long tradition. In a word, the perception is this: the enemy is on the right—conservative people, rich people, powerful people, and therefore Christians are not friendly. Republicans are not friendly. Democrats, on the other hand, are friendly. Liberals are friendly. There was a rather charming series of percentages that was published recently. Only 6 or 7 percent of American Jews think most or many Democrats or liberals are anti-Semitic. But 28 percent think Republicans are anti-Semitic, and 35 percent think most or many conservatives are anti-Semitic. About Christians, anywhere between 40 and 46 percent: Catholics, 40 percent; liberal Protestants, 42 percent; fundamentalist Protestants, 46 percent. This is extremely interesting, because who are Democrats but precisely Christians and blacks—and Jews think most or many blacks are anti-Semitic, and also conservatives. But some data show that there are more Democrats who call themselves conservative than call themselves liberal, though the plurality call themselves moderate or middle-of-the-road. So you have Democrats being considered friendly, but most of the people who are Democrats are unfriendly. This is a perception that is very strongly embedded in the minds of Jews. There does not even seem to be much generational difference in this regard."

Himmelfarb's friends-are-on-the-left view oversimplifies what Jews really think, said Charles Silberman. In fact, Silberman said, Jewish leaders and Jewish rank and file perceive different sets of friends.

"The congruence of opinion of Jewish leaders and rank and file holds for church-state issues, but it does not hold for a sense of who the friends and enemies are. In a 1981 survey there was an enormous discrepancy between leaders and rank and file. The leaders, by and large, had far more accurate perceptions of who was anti-Semitic or not, who was pro-Israel or not. Rank and file, for example, did not know that the trade union movement is pro-Israel and did not know that Congress is more pro-Israel than the White House. The leadership was far more accurate in terms of views of fundamentalists, far more accurate in terms of perceptions of anti-Semitism among Christians generally."

Himmelfarb then conceded some ground to Silberman, but just a little.

"You are right about leadership intellectually, but I do not think you are right about leadership in their gut. I was at a meeting not terribly long ago in which the crazy backwoodsmen in the Northwest, the Aryan Nation, were discussed. Someone suggested and put it forth as a possibility with a question mark that these people were encouraged by the religious, evangelical noises emanating from the White House. I consider that to be an infamous, demagogic statement. Yet it received a real round of applause. And these were precisely the kind of people who rationally and intellectually answered as they had answered in 1981."

Silberman, undaunted, responded by repeating that there is a "gap" between Jewish leadership and rank and file because of different perceptions of anti-Semitism.

"The gap does exist. It is the rank and file that cannot accept the argument that anti-Semitism is not a culturally significant factor. The leadership, by and large, accepts it. The visceral response comes out if certain buttons are pushed. But the distinction is there."

The perceptions of anti-Semitism will not soon die, conjectured Stanley Rothman, since "for some Jews anti-Semitism plays an almost necessary role. For some Jews and perhaps some of the Jewish leadership, the fear is that if anti-Semitism completely disappears then the Jewish community might erode or dissolve."

At this point in the conference discussion the author Lucy S. Dawidowicz placed an important historical note on the table by outlining the long view of Jewish-Christian relations in America. She argued that the Jewish community's friends are forever changing but that one thing does not change: the Jewish community's friends are determined in large part by who society's culturally ascendant groups are at any given historical moment.

"Many of the early Jewish settlers in this country were attracted to the dream of a universal brotherhood that would transcend their particular Jewish situation. The society changes, though. America itself undergoes a change, and the Washington-Jefferson outlook of universal brotherhood of no religious particularism changes. There are religious awakenings and great Christian revivals. In the 1840s and 1850s when there is a period of great Christian revivalism in the United States, there is a very young Jewish community, for the German Jews are beginning to come to the United States. And through the period of the late forties and late fifties there is an extraordinary amount of synagogue building. Jews in small numbers and small communities build very elaborate temples and synagogues. Why do they do this? It is interesting to follow the newspaper reports of the fundraising and the dedication and the opening of the synagogues.

"These small communities of Jews do not need a building. They do not need a synagogue. They need ten men in an inner room, where they can gather and do their own thing. But the Christian community is very much interested in Jews. It is another religion. Christians have finally met Jews, and they say, 'Ah, indeed, you do not have horns.' And, 'If you are a Jew, I would like to see how you are Jewish. What do you do to be Jewish? Where are your services?' There is in this Christian society in a period of revival great pressure on the small Jewish community to do its Jewish thing. Therefore, they start raising money to build this elaborate edifice that will show the Christians in their community that they are indeed practicing Jews. One always finds that they raise money from Christians, because they cannot do it on their own. At the synagogue dedication and opening ceremonies there are representatives of the Christian faiths, whatever they are in the community, and of the community leaders. The mayor comes. This is obviously the Jewish response to this Christian interest.

"This is what happened through American history. The Jews who feel any sense of Jewish identity will respond to what society is asking of them and be what is appropriate.

"When you have periods of rising or intense secularism in the United States, the balance shifts to those other groups. And I think there has been this kind of back and forth both in the larger American society and within the Jewish community of shifts in religiosity and observance, and secularism and nonobservance."

Then Dawidowicz brought her argument to bear on contemporary events.

"In the last forty years there has been a most dramatic change in every way in this country. If Jews have been more aggressive in terms of separation, it is because the society in which they live has also become extraordinarily secular. This is a hedonistic society. Think of it over the last thirty years: the transformation of American society in terms of morality and sexuality. It makes the days of the Model T look goody-goody. In this kind of a world obviously it is going to be the universalist kind of Jews who are going to be uppermost in the Jewish community and respond to what they think is in the society.

"And now that there is a new cycle entering in American history—complete with Christian revivalism, the rise of the evangelicals, and the return to religion among the population at large—many Jews are startled by what is happening. Jews are still startled by the changes that have occurred politically and socially and religiously in the last forty years and have been unable to come to terms with them, not only in terms of church and state but in terms of politics and everything else that has affected them."

Not speaking for the entire Jewish community, Milton Himmelfarb recalled less-than-fond memories from his boyhood, when he perceived a definitely ascendant group, the Archdiocese of New York, setting his personal Jewish agenda.

"I remember when I was a boy in New York. The powerhouse was down at 5th Avenue and 50th—the Archdiocese of New York. It was Cardinal Spellman who ruled New York. And how could you orient yourself if you hadn't picked up the *New York Times* that day? How did you know what to think? Well, if Cardinal Spellman said something, then you knew you were against it. And if Cardinal Spellman was against it, then you knew you were for it. That was the way you oriented yourself. It was a cheap, economical way of making up your mind." Needless to say, Himmelfarb added, "there has been a huge transformation from that."

Roman Catholicism having been mentioned, Michael Novak of the American Enterprise Institute, responding to the issue of anti-Semitism in America, introduced the similar case of anti-Catholicism in America.

"I could recount the same story that Morris Abram does in the letter to the *Washington Post* about being a Catholic student in a public school which was actually a Protestant school. About saying the Our Father not in a Catholic but in a Protestant way, about correcting the history teacher's spelling of a certain pope's name, about needing to get permission from the principal to be away for holy days (for I was an altar boy and needed to serve occasionally at a wedding or a funeral), about having an ambivalent reaction to the public schools. I worried both about the public schools' religiosity and their secularity. I found them not religious enough intellectually, but insofar as they were religious in prayer or allusion, I found them aggressively Protestant, even in a very sophisticated suburban school system.

"Anti-Catholicism is very deep in the United States. If you ask 'Is it good for Catholics?' there is no reason why everybody else should not ask

the reverse question, with the reverse purpose. What is the Enlightenment? What are you enlightened from if you are enlightened? You do not
have to be very sophisticated even in fourth or fifth grade to know it is
anti-Catholic—that is, it is enlightenment *from being Catholic.* And if
there is a Reformation, what is it that is reformed and what is it that is
corrupt? So the basic terms of discourse that you learn from a very early
age, if you are Catholic, are directed against your own identity."

Novak also suggested that, comparatively speaking, Catholics
might have taken more of a beating than Jews.

"By contrast and maybe this is a trick of perception, Jews have some
status in modernity. Being Jewish (insofar as being Jewish might mean
being more secular) gave Jews higher status the minute they went to
university. Because being modern, being not-religious, was better than
being religious. If you were religious, your professors tried to awaken you
from your unenlightened religiosity to enlightenment. In any event, I
have found that being Catholic means having less status than being
Jewish. I see it in the media, in the newspapers, in the intonations; I do
not see how one can avoid that feeling or sensibility."

To this Silberman offered what some (all except the Lutheran)
thought to be a joke. "When asked in a movie, 'Why do you always say
you're Jewish when you're three quarters Lutheran,' Walter Matthau
answers, 'Because I'm a social climber.'"

What Exactly Is Anti-Semitism?

Edward Dobson, editor of Jerry Falwell's *Fundamentalist Journal,* followed with a back-to-basics question.

"What is anti-Semitism? It's something that we all talk about, but
at least from the fundamentalist's perspective, I am really not sure what it
is. I know what anti-Catholicism is. As you well know, anti-Catholicism
has been a tenet within a substantial portion of the fundamentalist movement. We have probably been more anti-Catholic than anti-Jewish.
However, I perceive in the last ten years or so changes within fundamentalism. Issues such as abortion have brought us together. Through our
cooperative efforts we have reached a better understanding of each other.
Jerry Falwell has made very positive statements toward the Catholic
Church and toward the pope. I recently did an editorial in the *Fundamentalist Journal* declaring that anyone who calls the pope Antichrist has
missed the whole spirit of Christianity. All of this is new within the
fundamentalist movement.

"Is anti-Semitism a religious dogma? Is it a fundamentalist believing that Christ is the only way to heaven? Is it believing that I have an
obligation to proselytize, to preach this message? Does my desire to

convert others—and that includes all the peoples of the earth—mean that I am guilty of anti-Semitism?

"And how can we as fundamentalists prove that we are not anti-Semitic? Do we have to stop preaching the gospel? Do we have to stop going after people? Because if that is the criteria by which you are going to judge us, then I do not think there is any potential for dialogue or discussion or mutual understanding.

"This brings me to the bottom line of what I want to say: fundamentalists are a little afraid of the Jewish community. On the one hand, we are afraid that if we dialogue too much with you, we might like you. Then I think on the other hand there is a fear that somehow we may be contaminated by you, that somehow we will be less Christian because of our discussion, or perhaps you will be less Jewish."

Dobson's initial question evoked another question, this one by William Kluback of the Kingsborough Community College of the City University of New York. Directing his query to Dobson, Kluback asked, "Do you feel that the recent remark by a member of Strauss's party, the Bavarian party, that when German cash registers jingle Jews are immediately there, is an anti-Semitic remark?"

Dobson said, "I'm not sure. This is an example of a characterization that is incorrect and misperceived, but a common misperception within the fundamentalist community. There is the perception that Jews have all the money, all the power, and all the positions of influence. And I think that we as fundamentalists need to correct that misperception."

Himmelfarb also took a crack at the Kluback inquiry. Sure, that remark by the Bavarian party member and the misperceptions of fundamentalists could be considered anti-Semitic, he said, but that is because "anti-Semitism is a very loose word. It can even mean distance and discomfort." Certainly, as Dobson made clear, there is a pronounced distance between the fundamentalist community and the Jewish community, and the latter does tend to find anti-Semitisms in the former. But, Himmelfarb reminded the group, it is also true that the fundamentalist community tends to find anti-fundamentalist stereotypes in the Jewish community.

"Most Jews know very little about fundamentalists and fundamentalism. They certainly know very little about its theology. Jews have a stereotyped picture of the sociology of fundamentalism. Fundamentalists are good ol' boys who come from small towns in the South; they ride around in pickup trucks with rifle racks and they like to go hunting. It is a real style-of-life feeling of distance. Jews do not attend the same colleges that fundamentalists attend. The quintessential fundamentalist for Jews would be Elmer Gantry, if they had ever read the book."

Michael Novak then tightened the definition of anti-Semitism a bit, describing six basic types.

"I would like to walk through a number of differentiations regarding anti-Semitism. I will pick up the theme that anti-Semitism is usually defined loosely and that what one means right off the bat is giving offense and then let's go through some differences. With 'no offense' to Jack Cuddihy [author of *No Offense* (Seabury, 1978)] of course.

"First there is an element of ignorance. Sometimes you run into an ignorance that on the face of it is almost harmless; people can say things without knowing that they give offense, but that in itself can be offensive. Sometimes it is evident that they simply do not care or that they are not paying attention.

"A second kind of anti-Semitism involves something we often link with ignorance, but it is actually a little different—namely, the stereotype. I have learned in my own experience to distinguish between the stereotype which is offensive but true and the stereotype which is offensive and false. As I have become older I have come to think there is some truth in all stereotypes. It takes a little time and wisdom to admit that, but there it is. For example, Catholics on authority. There is a stereotype of Catholics as authoritarian and priest-ridden. There is truth in that. Catholics have a different view of authority and are preoccupied with authority in a way nobody else is. It is one thing we reflect when we refer to Catholics as practicing or not. One does not say that very often about Protestants, and actually it is not common to say it about Jews. Because Catholics are clear about authority, one often finds them citing the pope over against the bishops or the reverse.

"A third variety of anti-Semitism involves doctrine. All doctrinal identification is inclusive-exclusive: when we are for something, we are also against something else. This is a terrible and inherent problem in the relationship between Christianity and Judaism. In a way, acceptance of Christianity entails at least a partial rejection of Judaism, and one can say that there is in a way a certain anti-Semitism in Christianity. I would want to sort out the unfortunate doctrines that sometimes run rampant and are based on factual errors of many kinds—for example, attributing the death of Jesus not to the Romans but to the Jews. But when you get beyond such, there *are* some doctrinal differences. With respect to these, one might just as well say that Judaism is inherently anti-Christian.

"Fourth, there are also moral differences. Irving Kristol has a marvelous essay on the Christian temptation to gnosticism or other-worldliness, which becomes very clear on issues of worldly success or money. There is a terrible ambivalence in Christian culture on worldly success and money which is just irrational. And as far as I can see, it is not characteristic of other cultures. The jingling-of-money example reminds us of this: Christians are aware that Jews have a different attitude toward lots of worldly things, even pleasure. Sometimes Jews and Catholics are more alike in this; they have something in common that sets them apart from Protestants. But then moral differences can lead to a conflict of sensibility or offensiveness. One is just plain uncomfortable with the alien sensibility. Woody Allen on Catholics and sex is a good example. He knows that there is something different going on there. He does not always hit it exactly or without giving offense, but he never misses being funny about it.

"Fifth, there are the social differences. We are talking about status and infringement of identity. I never quite perceived the way Jewish infants and children would perceive Christmas until I saw it recently through some Jewish couples we are very close to. As they walked with their children, ages two to four, surrounded by Christmas, I saw something in a totally different way. The children were puzzled about why their homes didn't have the Christmas decorations they saw in the shopping centers; there were made a little nervous by it all because they didn't understand.

"Sixth, and finally, political differences can cause problems when power begins to get defined religiously. If you have to choose between a benign belief which is rather indifferent about beliefs and a passionate belief with directions you are not quite sure about, there will be a tendency to go with the more benign belief, the more secular-political expression. Since belief has a certain open-endness to it, a little nervousness about belief is inevitable.

"The reason I wanted to talk through these points is that some of them are irreducible. They are not anyone's moral fault necessarily, but they are going to present conflicting definitions. On the other hand, some of them can be changed and altered."

Among others, Rothman vividly described the worry of Jews over the "irreducibles" of anti-Semitism.

"There are primordial fears and anxieties in any society in which Christians speak about Christ and the importance of Christ and conversion and proselytizing people. The image, the unconscious gut image, is that this means they are going to kill us. To a great many Jews it means that they are going to kill us."

Naomi Cohen, who teaches history at Hunter College in New York, reinforced Rothman's point about Jewish worry over security matters.

"How do you convince American Jewry that they are safe, if in fact they are safe? I do not think that Jews can divorce our talk about religious identity or religious commitment from the fear or possibility of politicization, particularly since any idea in America historically can catch on only if it becomes part of the political agenda. That bears on security. Many nice Jews, and I would like to include myself among them, would agree with the Moral Majority on many things, and not just on Israel. But we are scared. What are we going to do if you decide that we have to behave according to some presumably Christian standard?"

Intending to lighten the discussion a bit, Charles Silberman wondered, "How do you persuade Jews that they are safe? Writing a book demonstrating that they are safe will not do it."

Howard Singer, a rabbi who has served at the Anti-Defamation League, was not so sure that Silberman had actually demonstrated the Jewish community's security in America.

"Not long ago I had dinner with seven others who had read Charles Silberman's book. Almost all disagreed with it. They were unhappy with the degree of safety and comfort that Silberman assigned to the Jewish community. They could not really pin down what it was they objected to in it, but the feeling that the book exaggerated the safety factor was very strong in that room. Later my wife and I concluded that for Jews today feeling safe is almost a form of disloyalty to Jewishness. We view safety almost with a survivor's mentality—with guilt. How dare we be safe? We do not have a right to safety. Quite aside from the objective situation, there was very definitely an identification of fear with a kind of loyalty to the essence of the historic Jewish predicament. Who are we to be different?"

This brought Singer back to the question about what constitutes anti-Semitism.

"The comment on jingling cash registers was in Jewish ears, minds and hearts an unquestionably anti-Semitic comment. You cannot possibly avoid it. And here sits a man, Ed Dobson, who is obviously not an anti-Semite but who does not hear it. He does not hear the anti-Semitism in that comment. That sends off warning bells in the Jewish heart and mind."

At this point, Milton Himmelfarb got out his red pen to make two corrections—regarding the apppropriateness of a word and the tense of a verb. *Fear* is not the correct word, he claimed.

"It is more 'apprehensiveness' or 'foreboding.' Also, there is a tense confusion in Jews' squabbles with Charles Silberman. Charles is using the present tense. His critics are thinking of the future tense. There is one thing that every Jew knows: Jewish history has been a succession of rises and falls. So you wait for the other shoe to drop. We are now on an upswing, but all of Jewish history guarantees that there will be a downswing. Look how great the German Jews once had it. Look how great the Spanish Jews had it in the Golden Age. And Babylonia. And Alexandria."

The whole discussion concerning the real and perceived friends of the American Jewish community led the participants to agree that the issue is far more interesting and complex than common assumptions

about the subject—namely that the friends are on the left and enemies
are on the right—would suggest.

A New Climate?

Is there now something new in American public life? Surely claims of
newness come down the pike of modern society all too fast and furiously
and should in general be received with more than a touch of skepticism.
And yet, perhaps new things do actually appear under the sun. Rabbi
Sobel anecdotally recounted recently spotting something new: a new
tone in Jewish-Christian—specifically Jewish-Roman Catholic—
relations.

"Two months ago I got a call late on a Monday afternoon. The
question was, 'Would you come to the White House next Friday to take
lunch with the President and eighteen other clergymen. The President is
about to depart for Geneva,' I was told, 'and the administration wants to
convey to these "leading clergymen" what the administration's major
positions are on the major themes, and simultaneously the President is
interested in what is on your mind.'

"There were nineteen of us there: the four active cardinal arch-
bishops—Krol of Philadelphia, O'Connor of New York, Law of Boston,
and Bernardin of Chicago; three rabbis—Israel Miller of Yeshiva University, the leading conservative rabbi Stanley Rabinowitz, and I; James
Kennedy, the Presbyterian; some Eastern Orthodox; and others. There
was no liberal mainline Protestant leadership there.

"There were briefings for an hour and a half from Richard Schifter,
the new Undersecretary of State for Human Rights; Sven Kramer, the
director of arms control for the Security Council; and others. The topics
were SDI [the Strategic Defense Initiative, or 'Star Wars'], the 'window
of vulnerability,' how the President was going to approach Gorbachev
with regard to human rights, and so forth.

"Then we go into the cabinet room for lunch. The President came
in, and it was very, very clear to me that by that time, nine days before his
departure for Geneva, whatever divergences of opinion there might have
been in the White House staff had now all coalesced. The President used
certain phrases that his experts had used.

"Fifteen minutes into the dialogue—and it really was a dialogue,
back and forth between the nineteen of us and the President—John
Cardinal O'Connor said, 'Mr. President, I hope that when you bring up
the issue of the repression of Soviet Jewry with Mr. Gorbachev, you make
it eminently clear that that issue, that appalling issue, is not only on the
agenda of the American Jewish community but that the issue of Soviet
Jewry is a major moral concern of the entire body politic.'

"About fifteen minutes later Bernard Cardinal Law said to the President, 'Although from reports we have read and heard the issue of the Middle East does not seem to be a priority agenda item for your conversations with Mr. Gorbachev, I do hope nevertheless, Mr. President, that you will have the opportunity to try to impress upon Mr. Gorbachev the important value of his bringing whatever pressure he can bring to bear on President Assad to at least enter in good faith an international conference, if such an international conference might be called, as a new initiative toward peace in the Middle East. But more importantly and hopefully, I hope that you will impress upon Mr. Gorbachev the high value and importance of persuading Assad to enter direct peace negotiations with the Israelis, as the Egyptians have done, so that Israel can know a peace and security that she has not known since her founding in 1948, and in the process we will be able to resolve the thorny issue of the Palestinians.'

"That two members—Law and O'Connor—of the most prominent of the Catholic hierarchy would address the President of the United States on these issues without equivocation when they could have spoken on a lot of other subjects, is a reflection of a new kind of climate."

Silberman detected something else that is new on the American scene. Jewish children today are "much more comfortable" with their Jewishness, he said. Though they are part of a minority, they feel neither bullied nor subtly pressured by the larger culture. An important component in the Jewish children's comfort, Silberman suggested, is the naked public square.

"One cannot separate that degree of comfort from the nakedness of the public square. That is not to say the public square should be permanently naked but that the de-Protestantization of the schools and American public life has been one of the critical factors in making Jews feel that they are members in American society rather than outsiders. The rational fear, as opposed to the irrational fear, is that whether intended or not the consequences of a more aggressive movement of religion into the public sphere is a return to the Protestantization or Christianization of public institutions."

So the issue is whether Jews should fear the new, somewhat aggressive entry of fundamentalists (the third new element in society) into the public square in America. Ed Dobson thought not, especially if the historical background of this entrant is taken into account.

"For many many years in this century, fundamentalists were indeed somewhat obscurantists—anti-intellectual, Appalachian, hillbilly types. We were very hesitant to enter into the political process, feeling that our calling and mission were somehow too sacred to be contaminated with the give and take of political dialogue and compromise. But in the late 1960s, for various social and moral and political reasons, fundamentalists felt very much like a threatened minority, felt that somehow the increasing secularization of society around us had now become a threat to our existence and to the values that we are concerned about and that to a great extent the Jewish community is concerned about. So in typical fundamentalist fashion, we bought into the idea of 'ready-fire-aim'! With little discussion or planning, we decided we must do something before our values were eliminated from the political process and before we ourselves might be eliminated. I do not mean elimination as extermination, but in terms of the whole society passing us by and leaving us with no influence in that society to advocate Judeo-Christian values. With the founding of the Moral Majority in 1979, we marched abruptly into the political process and recognized at least initially that we had considerable numbers. In the 1980 election we were perceived as having made a difference. Whether or not we actually did is highly debatable. But at least we got the liberal establishment's attention and spawned new organizations—groups that raised money based on our fundraising letters so that we could raise money based on their fundraising letters."

Dobson also gave assurances that fundamentalists are truly sorry for and have definitely learned from their sins of zealotry.

"Once you enter the political process, you have to accept some of the standards and criteria by which that process operates, one of which is negotiation and a willingness to be conciliatory. We do not have all the answers. We have made some fundamental and serious mistakes, for example, in our relationship with the Jewish community in the ways we have phrased and couched our concerns. Jerry Falwell has had the courage at certain points in his development to apologize for statements that have been made. We do not want to dominate the process, because if we dominated the process, then one day the process would dominate us. We want neither to dominate the political process nor to be dominated by it. We want to be legitimate participants in the pluralism of the American democratic tradition."

But still, Neuhaus warned, there is one legitimate reason for Jewish apprehension about the fundamentalist ascendancy in American life. That reason has to do with public philosophy—or rather, the fundamentalists' lack of such a philosophy.

"A few months ago," said Neuhaus, "the Center on Religion and Society sponsored a conference in Wheaton, Illinois, in which mainly evangelicals and fundamentalists took part. Ed Dobson was one of the participants. We addressed just this question of political philosophy, asking if there is any kind of underlying political philosophy in which the evangelicals and fundamentalists had related, in some conceptual manner, their religious commitment and its public implications to liberal democratic theory. One of the things that became poignantly evident is that there is no such conceptual framework. There is nothing comparable to Lutheran two-kingdom theory or Catholic natural law theory. All of these ideas are quite new to most of the evangelical/fundamentalist community. So here was a group with enormous perceived power at this particular moment in American life without any secure intellectual-conceptual working through of how power is to be related to truth in the political arena. That is one of the reasons why many Jews and others are nervous about people like that being in possession of power. They do not know what guiding or inhibiting principles are going to come into play if they exercise that power. Unless fundamentalist/evangelical political communities assemble such a political philosophy in the years ahead, that fear is going to continue to grow, because without it they are going to look like a loose cannon, conceptually speaking, on the deck of Western history's political thought and practice."

Marvin Wilson, who teaches at an evangelical college, was not persuaded that philosophy—political or any other kind—should be at the top of the evangelical/fundamentalist agenda with regard to the Jewish community. He urged that communitarian trust be placed above all else.

"The issue boils down to trust. We Christians have to earn the trust of the Jewish community. In the churches we need to do a better job of instructing about Jews, Judaism, the Jewish experience, and Jewish sensitivities."

It was suggested that such trust between the communities could be built more solidly upon deeds than words. To Richard Neuhaus this was yet another instance of trying to downplay the significant role of reason—and hence philosophy. He would have none of it.

"I would raise a question about whether it is less a matter of listening to what people say and more of watching what they do. I wonder if that is getting it backwards. I remember John Mitchell when he came in as U.S. Attorney General. Remember, one of the dumbest things he said was 'Don't listen to what we say, watch what we do.' The people he was trying to appease are much more impressed by what you say than by what you do. And similarly with regard to the agenda of the religious new right today. If you look at what that agenda actually is, what they want to do, it is eminently reasonable or at least it is open to discussion and debate within a democratic society. It is not terribly intimidating at all. The intellectual community, and especially the Jewish intellectual community, seem so much more impressed by somebody's ability to say it in a way that makes people feel safe."

Trust between evangelicals/fundamentalists and Jews, Neuhaus insisted, is not earned by deeds alone. It is also the product of reasonable discourse, which he seemed to imply might be possible—newly possible—in contemporary public life.

But if Jewish-Protestant trust is to be built on reason and knowledge, it cannot be expected to develop overnight, or in a month, or even in a year—for the simple reason that there is so little interreligious knowledge today. Wilson had spoken earlier about Protestant Christians' very limited understanding of the Jews and Judaism. Himmelfarb proceeded to tell a story to illustrate Jews' very limited knowledge of Protestant Christianity.

"What do Jews know about Christianity? Some years ago I was speaking at the University of Toronto about a related subject. A young Jewish man came up to me and said, 'I was a student at the university until a year ago. I graduated. Before coming to the university, I had had only Jewish friends and associates. I went to a Jewish day school. When I got to the university, my roommate was a Presbyterian. I remember asking him two weeks after we started living together, "What do Presbyterians *do?*"' That is to say, there are lots of physical things associated with being a Jew. A Jew rises in the morning, says proper prayers, and avoids doing certain things on Saturday—you don't carry money, you don't turn on the electricity, and so on. And Jews could understand Catholics. For example, on Friday in those days, they did not eat meat. It was doing something. But he was baffled: What do Presbyterians do? I do not think he ever got a satisfactory answer."

Still, contended David Novak, there is reason to hope and to strive for trust through deeds and discourse. At once realistic and idealistic, Novak said that there "can be a *modus vivendi* between Jews and Christians—even fundamentalists—in America, at least on certain levels. Granted, there will be tensions. But the fact is that Judaism has always thrived in societies that are intensely religious. It seems that Jews are not so threatened by a religious atmosphere in this society, provided that it is clearly understood that Jews will not simply knuckle under."

As should be obvious from the conference discussion up to this point, even in the face of an almost militant movement of evangelicals/fundamentalists into America's public square, the Jewish community is not about to "simply knuckle under."

JEWS IN RELIGIOUS, "SECULAR," AND POST-SECULAR (?) AMERICA

We had devoted most of our time to an exploration of current Jewish-Christian issues, but Jonathan Sarna was anxious to bring to the discussion the perspective and, possibly, the lessons of history. The discussion did take the direction he hoped, and yet this path led us predictably back to the concerns of the present and the future—specifically to certain religion-and-society problems and to what is alleged by some to be a crisis in American culture.

"Christian America"

In the beginning of America, Sarna began, were the founders. As might be expected, they were not of one mind concerning the role that religion might play in the society they were helping to shape. In fact, Sarna contended, they were of three different minds. Some of the founders "thought they were creating a Christian America, though what made it different was Protestant pluralism, which was an innovation. Others had in mind a religious America; that seems to be the tradition of the Northwest Ordinance. And the third group had in mind the great wall of separation." Understandably, said Sarna, "Jews appealed to the last two traditions, and appealed to the latter increasingly in the late nineteenth and twentieth century."

Despite the preferences of the Jewish community, however, the ideas of the first group, the Christian-America founders, gained the ascendancy late in the nineteenth century. During this period, "many of the Jews who spoke about America as a country where all religions should be equal and where freedom for religion should abound," Sarna continued, "found that some of the people they thought were their allies really were advocating Christian America. The revival that took place in the last quarter of the nineteenth century, not the one in the 1820s and 1830s, had a big impact on American Jewish thought. The resurgence of Christian-America thinking led many Jews to react by advocating a more secular-America viewpoint."

Several important but often unacknowledged points should be recalled about America's Christian-America period. First, as Protestant Christianity embraced American culture, Jews were increasingly excluded from mainstream society.

"The Jewish disenchantment with a religious America came at a point when the religious establishment, the Protestant establishment in America, totally identified with the culture," Rabbi Novak pointed out. "In other words, the notion was that to make it in America one had to be a Christian gentleman. This sort of religion was clearly deficient on Christian theological grounds, because it had lost what Reinhold Niebuhr used to refer to as the prophetic element of the critique of society. This is what the neo-orthodox theology of Niebuhr and Karl Barth criticized— the total identification of Christianity and culture that leads American Christians to view themselves as the vanguard of culture."

Novak went on to consider this historical problem in the present context.

"In the cultural climate now, with evangelicals and fundamentalists reasserting themselves, I see both a strength and a danger. I see a strength in the fact that fundamentalists and evangelicals have also been on the periphery of American society and were at many times its greatest critics. The danger that I see is that fundamentalists and evangelicals seem to be embracing conservatism with the same lack of critical judgment that some Jews and others exhibit in embracing liberalism. I feel most comfortable in a religious America where the religious establishment is pretty much a critic of culture. Not a mindless critic, not with the anti-Americanism of some types of critics. The good critic says the kingdom of God is not here, that it is not going to be brought about by human beings, and therefore we are going to have to participate and be in, but not of, the world."

Neuhaus, picking up on one of Novak's suggestions, raised a second, somewhat surprising point about Christian America—its strong connection to liberalism.

"All the talk about Christian America is very mainline talk, historically. It was the liberal Protestant denominations who talked about 'Christian America.' Jews and mainline Christianity were similarly liberal. Christianity, democracy, and socialism all went together in a Rauschenbusch or a Washington Gladden. They were all mutually reinforcing. It was definitely left of center on the political spectrum of American life."

Neuhaus went on to point out that "there was a secular version of Christian America with the same liberal presuppositions. It was a clear and attractive and apparently inexorably triumphant alternative to religious America. It was universalistic, secularistic, and modernistic in orientation."

Given the contest between religious liberalism and secular liberalism, Rabbi Novak found it easy to predict which would win and why: "When you have two versions of liberalism, one using traditional Christian language, however changed, and one using pure, straight secularist language, of course the secularist version is going to win. It's Occam's razor. There were too many assumptions on the religious side that you could cut out." It would be convenient to opt, he said, "for the purely secular side, hoping to cut out all of that underbrush and get down to the main agenda."

This led to a third point about Christian America—its demise and the Christian response to its demise. In this regard Charles Silberman observed, "Because of mass immigration at the end of the nineteenth century, mainline Protestants felt themselves to be an embattled minority in the same sense in which evangelicals and fundamentalists have in recent years. The temperance movement can be understood only in these terms, as a kind of symbolic politics. When you have lost power to the Irish in Boston, for example, you seek to control at least some aspects of behavior. At the base of the temperance movement was the need to stop these barbarians from drinking so much and debauching so much. The whole progressive movement was a reaction against the Catholic influx and the loss of control by the Protestant elite who saw themselves as fighting to save their values.

"When a group is losing real power, it moves from the objective to the symbolic to try to retain control by establishing values through legislation. When it controlled the society and its values, it did not need legislation to control behavior. Everyone followed the code that it established normally. It is when a group is no longer dominant that it needs to legislate morality."

But perhaps, it was suggested, the demise of the Protestant mainline's vision was not as disastrous and final as Silberman seemed to think. After all, during the twentieth century both Jews and Roman Catholics began defining themselves and viewing the world in increasingly Protestant terms.

Now that the idea of Christian America has been effectively dismissed from American public life, the lone exception being that it still lingers in the shadows of a few moral-majoritarian corners, where can a religiously based vision or public philosophy now be found? Jack Cuddihy offered one possibility: civil religion.

"Do you see civil religion as perhaps a means of trying to thread a way between the alternatives of a secular America, a religious America, and a Christian America?" Cuddihy wondered aloud.

Definitely not! answered several.

The Jewish critics suspected the Christian content of most civil religion. Milton Himmelfarb asserted that "Robert Bellah's opening shot in the civil religion debate—*Daedalus* in 1968—is a very *Christian* civil religion. He said that Washington is like Moses of the Old Testament who led the new children of Israel into their promised land. And Lincoln is like Jesus of the New Testament, because in bringing salvation to his people he was crucified. That is a charming piece of symbolism, or allegory, or whatever you want to call it. But it is certainly not civilly neutral about civil religion. It is a highly Christian perspective on civil religion."

Jonathan Sarna reinforced Himmelfarb's opinion.

"Some of the civil religion material is very strongly Christian. And after all, if Christmas is part of American civil religion, that suggests that civil religion is pretty Christian. Some of the writers on civil religion represent what we would call pan-Protestantism. Some people's civil religion is thoroughly secular. Some people's civil religion is religious without specifying religion. Some people's civil religion is really Protestant pluralism. We did not get far with civil religion because it does not have the kind of conceptual clarity that is necessary."

Civil religion may be conceptually confusing, Neuhaus agreed, but let us be conceptually clear about one point—civil religion is a *religion*.

"One of the difficulties of civil religion is that it assumes that people are going to buy into a new religion. A new religion is by definition, if one is a believer in a religion, a false religion. This includes civil religion. The response almost across the board, especially in the evangelical/fundamentalist community, to the civil religion proposition has been very reflective of that."

Before we get bogged down in the quagmire known as civil religion, Michael Novak interjected, we should remember some ground that both Jews and Christians share.

"There are some things that we take for granted that are so deep that we do not even see them. For example, the way in which, for Jews and Christians, the Bible has taught a narrative consciousness. It is always filled with suspense. At the beginning of a chapter you do not know whether King David will be faithful or unfaithful; and sometimes he will be one and sometimes the other. It teaches you to focus on the narrative side of human life and particularly on human will. That means we have a responsibility, as Jews and Christians, to change the world. That is, we believe that human will is very important and that history is changing. Most of our coreligionists in the world do not have that view. Hindus, Buddhists, and even Muslims have terrible difficulty adapting. This historical consciousness that we have gained together is very important."

To these commonalities Novak added the public nature of both Judaism and Christianity.

"Both Judaism and Christianity have a view of religion as public and as embodied. If either or both had the view that religion is invisible and private, our conference discussion would be so much easier. Then we would not care about the public symbols at all.

"There is an old ethnic joke. Heaven has British police, Swiss civil servants, Italian lovers, German mechanics, and French cooking. Hell is French civil servants, German police, Italian mechanics, Swiss lovers, and English cooking. Comparing this to our situation in America, I can say hell is militant unbelief—it is bad for Christians and bad for Jews— and militant religion—it's bad for both. But what is heaven? That is where things get vague. The reason things get vague there is the nature of the publicness of Christianity and Judaism.

"Jefferson wanted 'Israel' on the seal of the United States—the United States as a second Israel. It is when you try to embody religious claims in a way that can be seen or touched or smelled in a public ceremony that we—Christians and Jews—run afoul of each other."

The difficulty of publicly embodying religious claims and symbols in a way that is mutually satisfying to Jews and Christians just might be at the bottom of several contemporary Jewish-Christian-society problems.

Problems Galore

There are problems enough to be addressed in any discussion of religion and society, but when the conversation turns to *religions* in society, the number of problems awaiting comment increases dramatically. Take, for example, the case of the Ten Commandments and the public schools in Kentucky, Sarna challenged.

"You say, 'Wasn't it silly? Don't Jews observe the Ten Command- ments? Wasn't it foolish for the community to get involved in that issue? Why shouldn't the Ten Commandments be on the schoolroom wall? Why should anybody—especially Jews, who after all are supposed to cherish them—want to oppose it?' In the Midwest it was a very tough issue for a lot of people. When you look closely at that, it underscores the problems Jews have with admitting religion into, let us say, the public school."

The reason had to do with the Commandments as they actually appeared on the schoolroom wall. Sarna elaborated.

"First of all, the very order of the Kentucky version of the Ten Commandments is a Protestant order. Jews number them differently. The Jews start with 'I am the Lord thy God,' and the Protestants start with 'Thou shalt have no other gods.' What is done when one version is put on the wall is that subtly it is indicated that that reading of the Ten Com- mandments is right. Not only that, but translation is a problem. For example, 'Thou shalt not murder,' and 'Thou shalt not kill.' Once you put the Commandments on the wall, one of those readings has the official sanctioning of the government or the school committee. Even a case like this one, which one can argue should be an indicator of how religious America should work, shows that the Ten Commandments can become a subtle form of inculcating one group's view of what the Ten Commandments are. The poor Jewish boy, who learned in Hebrew school a different order and a different translation, is faced with that tension."

In jest Howard Singer proposed a solution: put the Ten Command- ments in Hebrew on schoolroom walls. Michael Novak had another idea:

"I would like to propose a creative political solution for the Ten Commandments problem that makes, I think, psychological sense. I think the Jewish position should be: in grammar school let it be the Jewish way, but in high school let it be the Protestant way. That way the kids will take out their rebellion on the Protestant establishment."

But this is no joking matter, declared Rabbi Novak. He recalled his experience in the public schools.

"We were taught by mainline, Protestant-type teachers, so we felt defensive. We felt that somehow, maybe, we were not really Americans after all. There was that image there. It was a clear put-down of every- body's ethnicity."

Dawidowicz then pointed out a problem that the Jewish communi- ty has in thinking through its role in American public life.

"One of the problems with the Jews in the history of America is that they have failed to make the distinction between the state and the society. This results in a wish to privatize religion so thoroughly that it seems not to exist in the society."

That might be one problem, Neuhaus urged, but the more crucial problem is related directly to the public school, which in fact is a government school.

"The problems arise so often in the schools, in the public schools, the government schools, where you have an illegitimate conflation of state and society—namely, that a social task—education—has been, for all kinds of historical reasons since the middle of the nineteenth century, part of the state. If one removes the school question, most of the others are not so urgent."

Though urgent, the public school issue is not the only problem the Jewish community confronts in America. There is also Christmas, which is hardly understood as a problem in the Christian community.

"Christmas is such a problem for Jews not just because they feel uncomfortable," Sarna explained, "but because it is the only American day on which Jews, who are after all equal Americans, feel somehow unequal. That is, it reminds Jews that maybe this is a Christian country and that they are somehow apart from it. How can Christmas be a national holiday, if there truly is church-state separation? If you call Christmas secular on the other hand, as some do, why shouldn't all Jews have Christmas trees? This is something most rabbis will not accept. Rabbi Sobel's predecessor at Temple Emanu-El was in the forefront of the battle to put Christ back in Christmas. Why should he care? The point is that Christmas is a Christian holiday, and not an American day. And yet there is a national Christmas tree and a national proclamation.

"Now there are some who would say 'Let's have a national Hannukah menorah opposite that. If this is a religious America, then you should have a national Hannukah menorah, and the Orthodox Church should have a lighting of the Christmas tree twelve days later, and so on.' Advocates of a separationist agenda, on the other hand, say we should not have a Hannukah menorah in Central Park or a Christmas tree or any of the other. The question is what is better, and where do you draw the line? Are we going to let the Moonie symbols come in? And if not, why not? And the same problem arises in the school: What is legitimate, and what is not?"

Yet another problem that Jews must contend with resides in their own community, perhaps in their own hearts and minds. Himmelfarb spoke to the problem of a pesky Jewish ideology.

"There is a kind of ideologism coexisting with prudentialism in the breast of each Jew. In the Jewish community there is a consensus that says No to the Christian right and Yes to blacks. I do not think that is prudentialism. I think it is an ideology. It is a deep emotional commitment. What damned difference does it make for advancing the cause of 'reproductive freedom,' as the phrase has it? (By the way, reproductive freedom in the United States is like religious freedom in the Soviet Union. In the Soviet Union religious freedom means freedom from religion; and in the United States reproductive freedom means freedom from reproduction.) Really, what difference does it make in the actual availability of abortion if the Union of American Hebrew Congregations passes a resolution or does not pass a resolution or even testifies before a congressional subcommittee? What practical difference does it make? On the other hand, look at the practical benefit from *not* testifying. You do not irritate Catholics needlessly. You do not irritate an awful lot of Americans who hate abortion. So shut up, organizations. Do not come out antiabortion. Just shut up. No, the need to *testify*, if I may use that word, is so strong that Jews are counterprudential. There has been a lot of prudentialism, but increasingly there has been less prudentialism and more ideological passion."

But why is there all of this ideological passion and/or passionate ideology, particularly in American Jewish organizations? Singer floated one (not very nice) possible explanation.

"I think it can be reduced intelligently to a certain bureaucratic need on the part of very small people to look big. When very small people stand on the shoulders of big organizations, they look like giants. They are, nevertheless, pygmies. And this is a key to the Jewish community: for the last fifty years very small people with very small brains and even smaller souls have been standing on the shoulders of enormous organizations."

In the wake of this statement, Marvin Wilson insisted that we must be charitable. It could be that the Jewish "leadership, the theoreticians, are a decade ahead of where the grass roots are," he said. This point sounded vaguely familiar to those who have listened to some ecumenical and mainline agencies defend their programs in the face of criticisms from their constituencies.

And finally, there is another problem in Jewish community affairs—Jewish identity. What does it mean to be a Jew? Most people know what it means to be a Roman Catholic, and most know, more vaguely, what it means to be a Protestant. But Jewish identity is something else. Irving Louis Horowitz of Rutgers University contributed three categories through which Jewish identity might be better understood.

"Jewish identity can be very national without being religious; it can be cultural without being national or religious; and it can be communitarian without being cultural, national or religious. Identification in the Jewish world is radically different from identification in the Christian world, because one is not dealing with a unified system that is found in

New Testament belief. Therefore, the character of what is public in Jewish life is not the same as the character of what is public in Christian life. Its public character can be national and highly secular. It can be religious and public and at the same time it can be national and have a strong identification with Israeli forces and be entirely theistic. Some Jews have a very low level of religious commitment or belief and yet have a very high level of Jewish commitment in terms of the Israeli experience. The public nature of being Jewish and the public nature of being Christian cannot be dealt with in a unitary fashion. One needs a kind of trinitarianism to explain the character of Judaism. One has to see it in terms of the religious experience, the national experience, and the cultural experience. These experiences may not involve the same publics, and they may have a very low level of overlap except in moments of identification by others—for example, under Nazism, when the identification was not simply self-made but was made for the Jews by the Nazis. So the unity at times is imposed unity. The unity within Jewish life is parceled out differently than in Protestant culture and Catholic culture in American life."

Horowitz went on to conclude that "One cannot take for granted the religious context of the Jewish experience and see other elements as peripheral to that context. That is not the way to get at the question of Jews in an unsecular environment."

Ronald Sobel pointed out an absurdity here: "After four thousand years of nothing short of miraculous continuity and survival, at best the two greatest Jewish scholars of any generation will be able to define for only a minority of the Jewish people the answers to two fundamental questions: Who is a Jew? and What is Judaism? This is an existential absurdity!"

With all of these conflicts and ambiguities swirling inside the Jewish community and between the Jewish community and the greater society, some Jews lust after some solutions somewhere. So they try to "settle" selected issues, sometimes in the courts. David Novak, who spoke to this fact of Jewish life in his conference paper, reiterated it here. There is an approach that involves "a fundamentalism of American law," he said.

"In other words, it is basically the idea that somehow social disputes and social questions are solved juridically, that once the court has ruled, everything should simply follow in its wake. That has proven to be false. Furthermore, it is simply a bad reading of American history. Look at the abortion debate. No matter how you stand on that debate, anybody who thinks that *Roe v. Wade* settled the issue in 1973 is wrong. It was not settled. It was exacerbated. Questions of segregation, questions of separate-but-equal treatment are other examples. I consider this almost a misplaced literalism, a literalism that would no longer be acceptable if it was based on a literal reading of the Bible but was subsequently applied to the American juridical system."

According to Novak, fundamentalism—juridical or otherwise—is not the best response to the tensions that exist inside and outside the American Jewish community today.

American Culture in Crisis?

With the saying "If it ain't broken, don't fix it" in mind, Stanley Rothman issued a series of important questions.

"Before we decide what we want to put back in the public square, we have to reach some agreement about what has worked there and why it has worked. Most basically, is something broken? And if something is broken, what exactly is broken? And how are you going to try to fix it?"

These questions—especially the matter of whether anything is actually broken—directed the remainder of Monday afternoon's discussion toward various comments on the alleged crisis in American culture.

Since he had raised the questions, Rothman also took a crack at answering them. He began with what almost amounted to cheerleading.

"I believe that America has been working for a couple of hundred years, which is not a very long historical period. Despite the fact that many Jews have had a rough time in America, generally America has been quite receptive to Jews and has done a lot of things that Jews find very satisfactory. After all, by 1956 Jews had the highest per capita income of any group in this country. It has worked partly because of the Protestant orientation which founded it and out of which sprang the liberal individualism which was based on that."

Then he became a bit more restrained.

"There is a feeling that as this liberal individualism erodes and changes, some of the good things about America may be in the process of being undermined and that we do not know what to do about it."

Novak went directly to what he perceived to be broken in American culture.

"What is the cultural crisis? One of the things the 1960s did was to attack the bourgeois, essentially English culture and morals and to shipwreck the left. You suddenly had a dominant motif that was adversarial, almost purely adversarial. Insofar as it had anything affirmative to say, it was utopian, flower-child type of talk."

But this crisis need not be considered a permanent fact of American culture, Novak implied, for there is an intellectual movement with deep religious and philosophical currents that is coming to the rescue.

"What is the movement coming in behind that that seems to have the most staying power? It is called neoconservative. One characteristic of neoconservative thought that is understated—because people interpret it politically—is the degree to which it is fundamentally an ethical and a religious movement. It is characteristic of all the neoconservatives that they have regained a religious sensibility and think that religion is terribly important. Moreover, they turn to the English tradition. Neoconservatives are really old liberals, but they are old liberals in a Burkean sense: they believe in the importance of liturgy, community, ethnicity, and roots, not atomic individuals. They have a sense of community, prayer, religion, and the rest of it.

"Remember that the neoconservative movement is led in large measure by Jewish intellectuals. It may turn out to be the case that fifty or one hundred years from now the neoconservative reinterpretation of the American experience will be the one that sticks. It may be put on a more sound basis than it was in the past, philosophically speaking. There is a dissatisfaction with reading John Stuart Mill's, John Rawls's, and others' interpretations of American institutions. Something there does not ring true: they imagine an atomic individual putting all this together by contract; they completely devalue family, neighborhood, ethnic ties, and covenant. The neoconservatives remember these."

Novak also noted that whereas the "Christian America" vision was the product of Protestant thought, the public vision emerging from neoconservative circles is the product of Roman Catholic and Jewish thought. Ironically, some of those relatively new to the American experiment seem most dedicated to preserving, refining, and advancing it.

Listening to this, Richard Neuhaus had grown very impatient. He was not convinced that the group appreciated the gravity and depth of America's cultural crisis.

"I am extremely skeptical of intellectuals who are paid to be crisis-mongers, who constantly proclaim new problems so people will pay them to explain the new problems and hold some conferences and generate some more problems and hold more conferences and publish more books and so on. And yet in this context *crisis* is the right word. I think something is broken now that has not been broken since the launching of the modernity project. The problem is that we can no longer discuss the good in public. That is where we are. We are at a point that Ernest Fortin of Boston College calls 'nihilism without the abyss.' In other words, a lot of people look and say, 'We aren't yet in the abyss. Look, all the horrible things aren't happening yet.' But they do not realize that the premises on which we are operating are an invitation to abyss, as clearly as anything can be.

"The issue of abortion, which is terribly important in itself, is emblematic of a crisis as severe as any society can undergo. When you cannot as a society deliberate about who belongs to the community for which you accept shared responsibility, when you surrender that question to the technicians as *Roe v. Wade* does, society is in crisis.

"The Jewish community, along with the black community, is the most perduring, identifiable, vulnerable minority in American society. Without detracting from Charles Silberman's rather upbeat reading of the current state of anti-Semitism, I think the seeds of anti-Semitism are now present. One does not have to be a Rosemary Radford Ruether to recognize that there are some embedded sources for the generation and promulgation of anti-Semitic passions.

"If we cannot define the good, then we cannot define absolute evil. That is the point where we are in public: we cannot talk about good and evil. And if one cannot talk about good and evil in public, one cannot talk about the evil of anti-Semitism. And that too can finally go the route of the technical solution reinforced by the perceived interests of a demagogically inflamed majoritarianism.

"For all these reasons, I think something is broken, very fundamentally. I do not think in modern Western civilization—or in Western civilization generally, going back to Athens and Jerusalem—that there has ever been a point at which anybody representing the highest level of deliberation in the society has said, like the U.S. Supreme Court said in 1973, that the philosophical and religious and traditional beliefs and practices of the society cannot be permitted to impinge upon the question of who is protected as a human being. I do not think National Socialism asserted it that clearly. I think something is really broken. And to allude to the fact that it keeps on working in some kind of day-by-day way—we get our paychecks, and there's food in the supermarkets, and nobody is out to kill us—and to appeal to that for comfort is whistling in the dark. Because unless it has some kind of moral premise, it is not going to work very long."

By the end of this homiletical intervention, the group was convinced—or largely convinced—of the crisis.

Fine. So there is a crisis. But where do we go from here? Rabbi Sobel broke the crisis-inspired silence and talked eloquently about the need to turn a new page.

"Jews are 'the people of the book,' and we are about to turn, because of the crisis, to a new page. And I suspect that for a variety of reasons, while thinking about the things that have tended to cement Jewish identity at least since the end of World War II—a Holocaust consciousness and, more profoundly, the phoenix rising out of the ashes, the state of Israel. We are choking already on too much attention on the Holocaust. Holocaust, Holocaust, Holocaust! And frankly, internally the Jewish people cannot afford significantly and meaningfully to define themselves in terms of the Holocaust. If the Holocaust becomes the centrality of our existence, this is a distortion of Jewish life.

"So we come to that next page. And what we see is a *tabula rasa*, what Richard Neuhaus calls the naked public square. If that page is to be filled, and we are going to have to write it, then for a whole variety of reasons the crises of modernity in the latter part of the twentieth century are going to have to be addressed in religious terms—not exclusively, but at least dominantly."

Rabbi Novak agreed. He went on to outline how the Jewish community might act as a model in helping American culture to attempt to resolve its rather ominous crisis. Judaism's model is halakhah.

"The basic issues that are before our society at the present time are questions of normative ethics: abortion, the question of how much money should be spent on the poor and how much money should be spent on arms, and what have you. This is an area where for the first time, probably, in history, there is a beginning interest on the part of the general society to understand what the greater part of Jewish time and energy was devoted to. And that was the halakhah. Professor Ginsburg many years ago said that of the books in the British Museum by Jews, seventy-eight percent were about halakhah.

"There is not in Judaism what one could call theological ethics—that is, an ethic deduced from theology. There is a theology, and there is an ethic, and then there are all kinds of interrelations between them. Now that is precisely what we are dealing with in America today. We are dealing on the one hand with practical experience which is represented primarily in the whole constitutional history. On the other hand, does that mean that one has totally to suppress where one comes from? Does one have to go back to John Rawls's 'original position,' which is a total fiction? The Jewish tradition is marvelous: in the halakhah you have to present arguments that are based on precedent, common sense, and so on—arguments that are informed by theology but not deduced from theology. The Jewish model is that you do not deduce from one principle; instead you bring in five different principles and you play them off against one another. Here practical judgment has a much greater role than some kind of preconceived metaphysical model. For the first time the non-Jewish world is interested in what Jews have been devoting so much time and energy to."

Michael Novak then tried to imagine how Rabbi Novak's lesson on halakhah might be worked out in the currently naked public square.

"The opposite of a naked public square is not a clothed one. Instead, the image is between a silent and an oral one. That is to say, when the public square is filled with argument, when every person is willing to testify religiously in public, and when a pluralist public is enlivened by that debate, that is the opposite of a naked public square. And the model for that is more obvious in Jewish experience than anywhere else—in the Jewish meeting. The Jewish meeting is full of more forthright argument than you will find in any comparable meeting around. In my experience no other group of people is more articulate or explicit about a whole range of presuppositions and differences than the Jewish community."

The American Jewish community has lived through the era of the Christian public square and is now living through the crisis of the naked, or silent, public square. It is possible, though not certain, that the Jewish community could publicly employ some of its skills, virtues, and vision for the good, and for the good of American society. If this is done, the public square of American society would probably be a noisier but less crisis-ridden place.

CHRISTIANS PERCEIVING JEWS

Stepping into the pulpit, so to speak, Marvin Wilson introduced the conference's third paper like many preachers introduce their sermons— with a telling joke.

"A rabbi and a Presbyterian minister had spent an afternoon together. When it came time to say goodbye, the Presbyterian waved and said, 'Keep the faith!' The rabbi waved and replied, 'Keep the Commandments!'"

Some of those present chuckled but thought it important to keep both the faith and the Commandments.

Perhaps Wilson later regretted this beginning, for a spirit of light-heartedness persisted as he attempted to be a bit more sober.

"It has been written that Judaism needs Christianity as an ally against the paganization of our civilization. There have always been Jews looking for Christianity to be a partner in the battle against the secularizing process."

At this point Neuhaus quipped, "I wish that we had the paganization of our society! 'Up to paganism' would be a marvelous motto for the renewal of American society."

And David Novak added that "It has been said that the reason monotheism has a certain attraction to secular liberalism is that one is the closest whole number to zero."

Wilson persevered through the buffets of humor to get back to his point.

"Judaism has rightly been characterized as a religion of optimism, and this has been passed to Christianity. No matter how bad things may appear to get and how naked the public square may appear to be, both communities of faith can affirm that history is not going in circles but is moving toward a definite goal and a glorious climax."

Optimism is but one of the things that the Christian community perceives in the Jewish community. It also sees the present Jewish community as a reminder of historical Christian anti-Semitism, as a community that can, rightly or wrongly, be charged with "dual loyalty," and as a community that is caught in the midst of an alleged American cultural realignment.

Legitimate Christian Guilt?

For centuries Christendom has been anti-Semitic in spirit and in action. That is common knowledge. But the question is whether contemporary Christians should feel a legitimate guilt? Wilson answered with a resounding Yes. Not only do Christians need to know that they are in a sense guilty, but also they need to repent.

"Anti-Semitism is a spiritual problem. I do not believe that education alone will solve this problem. And that is why at the conclusion of my paper I stress the need for the church to come to grips with repentance. For two thousand years the church has stuck its bony finger in the Jew's face and said, 'You repent!' but I am not sure the church has faced up to the issue of the need for its own repentance. The very denial of God's sovereign choice and election of the Jewish people to be the vehicle of divine revelation to the world, the refusal to accept that notion of election, is a kind of anti-Semitism."

Neuhaus was not so sure about Wilson's call to repentance. Nor was he sure about the Christian Clergy Task Force on Anti-Semitism, a Boston area group in which Wilson participates to combat anti-Semitism.

"Is a response like that of the Boston task force a constructive thing, generally? Let me be provocative about it. Doesn't it intensify what some Christians and a few Jews are beginning to say—that there is an artificiality in Jewish-Christian relations at this point, an artificiality created by an enormous imbalance in terms of 'degradation rites' and information? The message seems to be that the primary obligation of Christians is to jump through the hoops of self-degradation and that this somehow strengthens Jewish-Christian relations. Is that in fact the case? Is there an imbalance on the information side of it, in that it is assumed that Christians have an obligation to learn a great deal about Judaism, and there is very little obligation on the part of Jews to learn about Christianity?"

Rabbi Novak offered the first Jewish opinion on the issue of Christian guilt.

"Anti-Semitism has been a Christian problem. But it has not been an exclusively Christian problem. We cannot reduce anti-Semitism to Christianity, even though there have been Christian manifestations of anti-Semitism."

Still, in Novak's opinion Christian anti-Semitism poses a special problem.

"I am extremely suspicious of people like Rosemary Ruether. This is why. I think there is a phenomenon in the Jewish-Christian dialogue that can be called Christian self-hate. Now we all know what Jewish self-hate is. We have seen a lot of varieties of that. But in some radical types of Christian theology—the types that say 'Let us root out evil and get right back to the gospel'—I find this an attempt by people who were raised in Christianity or who formally have a Christian commitment to use anti-Semitism as a battering ram against their own origins. Basically, they attempt to transcend their own Christianity. Reuther's latest work is really anti-Christian, over and above her work on anti-Semitism. Hans Küng looks orthodox compared to her. I am quite suspicious of that, for I prefer Christianity to secularism and other *isms*. Christians have to work out their own tradition, have to think about ramifications, have to emphasize some things and deemphasize other things. Every religious tradition that is alive and continually making judgments has to do that. The fascination of some in the Jewish community with varieties of Christian self-hate is extremely damaging. For Jews to ask Christians to de-Christianize Christianity is an outrageous demand and serves no good purpose whatsoever."

Neuhaus was again provocative.

"Is it accurate and constructive for Christians to view the Holocaust and what it represents as their crime, qua Christians? Should Christians continue to think about their relationships to Judaism through the spectrum of guilt for the Holocaust?"

Ready with an answer was Milton Himmelfarb. He advocated moderation in all things—even guilt.

"What do we tell ourselves about guilt and Holocaust? I have a near-idiotic rule of thumb. It is the old parents' creed: 'Go see what the children are doing, and tell them to stop.' I would suggest that this applies across the board. If there are Christians who wallow in guilt, then they are enjoying their guilt too much. As a good ascetic, I believe that people should not be allowed to enjoy themselves too much. The same applies to Jews. For some peculiar combination of reasons there are many Jews who wallow in Holocaust guilt. That is wrong. If there are Jews who completely ignore the Holocaust on the other hand, then they should be told to stop ignoring it. But for others, for whom it has become the central meaning of their Judaism, tell them to stop!"

And while you are at it, Himmelfarb implied, tell them to stop trivializing the Holocaust.

"The great danger of Holocaust is demagogy and easy transitions and substitutions. For example, at the time of the teachers' wars in New York City about twenty years ago, there were neighborhood-control people who were screaming about 'the holocaust' visited upon them in the schools of Brooklyn. Of late, it has also been directed against Jews.

Jews themselves, for several years now, have been accused of holocaust. Bishop Tutu implies that there is an Israeli complicity in 'the holocaust' of the South African government against the South African blacks. Although liberation theologians do not use the word, they implicitly accuse the West of committing a holocaust, or genocide, against the South; since Israel is of course part of the West, Israel must be generically genocidal as well as specifically genocidal."

Rabbi Novak suggested that a little historical analysis was in order.

"Consider this proposition: the responsibility for the Holocaust, the war against the Jews, can be directly laid on Christianity. Now, look at some of the facts. There are three strands of Christianity, basically— Catholic, Protestant, and Orthodox. Let's look at the record. Catholic Italy—enormously impressive acts of saving Jews. Catholic Poland— very unimpressive. Protestant Denmark, Lutheran Denmark—very impressive. Lutheran Germany—very unimpressive, needless to say. Orthodox Bulgaria—extremely impressive. Orthodox Ukraine—abominable. The question is what kind of theological sense we are to make out of those facts, which are indisputable. We are trying to establish some sort of relationship between theology on the one hand and ethics/politics on the other."

And here Judaism, Novak reiterated, can be especially valuable.

"Judaism produces a paradigm of interrelationships between theology and ethics: religious values and a religious stance have definite ethical ramifications without ethics being deduced from theology. In other words, there are certain basically ethical/political arguments which can stand on their own feet, at least initially, however they need a broader perspective."

Novak proceeded to apply Jewish ethical methodology to issues that often generate Jewish and Christian guilt—the death of Jesus and the Holocaust.

"We have to deal with crimes against the Jews on ethical criteria and not automatically on theological criteria. That, primarily, is what we Jews have always said. For example, on the question of deicide, we are perfectly willing to admit the fact that some Jews were involved in the unjust murder of Jesus of Nazareth. But that does not entail guilt on my part. Visiting the iniquity of the fathers on the children in Jewish theology, specifically, is divine and mysterious; every man dies for his own sin, not for somebody else's."

Finally Novak called for Christians to jump off the Holocaust-guilt bandwagon and for Jews to let them jump off.

"If we Jews have argued this way against the deicide charge for generations, we cannot pull the same kind of logic on Christians. Therefore, political/ethical argumentation that is related to theological discussion is required. The notion of saying that this crime, the Holocaust, is the direct result of, was caused (incidentally, the original word for *cause* in Hebrew and Greek meant 'guilt') by, Christianity is morally illegitimate."

Then it was Lucy Dawidowicz who spoke as a historian on the question of Christian guilt for the Holocaust.

"I first was made painfully aware of Christian guilt during the Eichmann trial, when I read the responses in the Christian press to what was happening. At best it was a kind of breast-beating—'Alas, we are all guilty. Man is a sinful creature. He has great capacity for evil. And we all harbor evil thoughts in our minds which are not unike these terrible deeds.' It was very disheartening for anyone who was looking for people to understand what really happens in the world and to understand what happened in Germany to get this kind of response. It shows no under-standing of the political events and the kind of thinking that led to the murder of the European Jews. This kind of generalized, vaporized 'We are all guilty for everything' is not based on factual evidence."

Neuhaus agreed by replying with what sounded like a principle: "A sentimentally generalized guilt leads to an evasion of guilt."

According to Dawidowicz, guilt is always related to historical acts and events, which involve responsible (that is, able-to-respond) people.

"If you are guilty for something, you have to be responsible for a certain act that you have committed. Now when you are an historian, you study specific events and you know that these events have happened because of human intervention (that is, if you are not a determinist)—people did certain things, people are responsible for their actions, they gave orders, they said things, they carried them out, and so on. The National Socialist German state conceived, organized, planned, and carried out the murder of six million Jews. It is likely that this could not have happened without centuries of Christian anti-Semitism that had made it possible for Germans and other people in different European countries to listen to what the National Socialists were saying and to think that they were saying the same old kinds of things against the Jews. There was present a certain kind of acceptance and receptivity. But I do not believe that the Christian church can in any form be held responsible for the ideas of the National Socialists and how they carried out that murder.

"Where there is evidence of complicity—in Germany or in Slov-akia or any place else—you have a specific event with specific people responsible for specific actions. Therefore, you have responsibility. And therefore, yes, you can attribute guilt. On the basis of historical truth, it is wrong for Christians to carry guilt for the Holocaust."

After Charles Silberman asserted that the majority of American Jews do not want guilt from the Christian community over the Holo-caust, and after it was acknowledged that it is unhealthy for communities to relate to each other on the basis of guilt, Rabbi Sobel consented and sharply recast the points made.

"Repentance is not really what the Jewish community wants or expects from the Christian community. One of the things I think we want is for Christianity to undo, as Edward Flannery says, a great deal of what Christendom has done. Those pages of history, in Flannery's *Anguish of the Jews*, which Jews have committed to memory are the very ones that have been torn from Christian and secular history books.

"The idea that Christians—even in this room—somehow bear a responsibility for what some Christians did to Jews in Spain in 1492, in Poland in 1648, in Germany in 1939, is as irrelevant and morally reprehensible as the idea that all Jews are responsible for the role that some Jews may or may not have had in the death of Jesus. That has got to be said clearly, and honestly.

"For someone to grovel at my feet demeans that person's humanity, and it demeans my humanity. Any effort to make that the basis of a healthy relationship between Christians and Jews is doomed from the start. It is absolutely doomed.

"What Jews want from Christians is not so much repentance as the process of looking at those pages and studying them."

Marvin Wilson agreed that those torn-out pages of history must be replaced, read, and studied by Christians. But, he suggested, this reading just might lead to the sort of repentance he was talking about.

"When I define anti-Semitism and the need for repentance, I am not suggesting groveling. That is not what repentance means. Anti-Semitism is a spiritual problem. It has its roots in this affront to God, this hubris in the face of God's authority, by not accepting what the Scriptures say about the Jew. Its cure involves repentance, a perfectly good term. It is a Jewish term. It simply means to forsake wrong and return to the living God for a new beginning. Here Christians need to understand the pages of history that many omit. One is not going to repent of anything of which one does not understand the history."

The issue during this segment of the conference was guilt. Is there guilt in the Christian community for the sins of anti-Semitism and the crimes of the Holocaust? If there is, should there be? If there is not, should there be? Obviously, the conferees did not reach a consensus on this question. But they did hold in common one assumption: Christian guilt (or its absence) with regard to Judaism and Jews should not escape critical examination. Nor should the charge of "dual loyalty," which was the next topic of the day.

Jewish Dual Loyalty—Fact or Fiction?

At this point in the discussion Jack Cuddihy made an offhanded comment about the alleged split or dual national loyalty of Jews. "There is this ancient canard of dual loyalty, which has been so easily and deco-

rously buried but which comes back," he said. At the time of the conference, the issue was receiving attention again in connection with the
case of Jonathan Pollard, a Jew who was caught spying in the United
States for Israel.

Milton Himmelfarb traced the origins of dual loyalty to the eigh-
teenth century.

"At the time of the French Revolution there was the notion of a
nation within a nation, which was not necessarily pejorative. It was a
factual statement that the Jewish community in France was a nation
within a nation. It was in but certainly not of the society. As the nineteenth century progressed, the expression changed a little and became a
little more sinister. What had been applied to the Jesuits in the eigh-
teenth century as a state within a state (and here I paraphrase Jacob Katz)
in the later nineteenth century began to be applied to Jews in their newly
emancipated state of civil equality."

Himmelfarb went on to describe the nasty turn that the dual-
loyalty problem took.

"A German philosopher and Social Democrat about a hundred
years ago accused German Jews of a swindle. That is to say, they had not
kept their side of the bargain, of the implicit contract that had been signed
when Emancipation was graciously conferred on them. Their part of the
bargain was to be good Germans. But they were not good Germans. They
had a dual loyalty. For instance, he said, suppose there were charitable
appeals among German Jews for Russian Jewish victims of pogroms and
for German Christian workers suffering from unemployment. If a German Jew were to hesitate for a moment before saying that his primary
duty is to give money for the relief of the unemployed German Christian
worker, if for a moment he were to hesitate and think that perhaps he
ought to direct that money more to Russian Jewish victims of pogroms,
the philosopher believed, then that would show him to be guilty of dual
loyalty, and that guilt would constitute proof that he entered into the
contract with an intention to swindle.

"The notion of dual loyalty ultimately goes back to a certain impa-
tience or incomprehension over the fact of continued Jewish particularity. Obviously if Jews, as a small minority, are to continue to survive at
all in the world, then prosperous German Jews must feel that their moral
obligation is to assist in the relief of persecuted Russian Jews. If you deny
them that right, if you say that this in itself is a swindle, then you in fact
are denying the right of Jews to continue existing in their particularity.

"Along comes 1948 and now you have a specific state, Israel, so
that dual loyalty can now be a much more concrete question than before.

"The very formulation of 'dual loyalty,' as can be seen from its
origins, is implicitly a grave reservation about the continued right of the
Jewish people to exist in their particularity. Implicitly it supposes that

national loyalty must lead to the dissolution and disappearance of the Jewish community."

Over the decades Zionism has labored to insure the protection of Jewish particularity, Steven Katz asserted, and yet it does not raise the problem of dual loyalty.

"The primary concern, the raison d'être of Zionism is justice. Zionism assumes that there is an imbalance of power in the world, a world organized according to nation-states, and that the Jewish people, without some fair degree of power, will always be sacrifices on the altars of the nations, for whatever reasons. Zionism is an attempt to solve the problem of powerlessness. With power comes the converse—the phenomenon of spying and so on. Power brings its warts. But it doesn't raise the specter prima facie of dual loyalty if one understands that the defense of Zionism and Israel is the articulation of a cry for justice. The Jewish people cannot achieve justice in the world, created as it is, without a state. That has been shown over and over again to be the case.

"Zionism is an antieschatological and antideterminist phenomenon. It is based on the premise that history is open. That is, Zionism is against historical closures."

Neuhaus detected what he thought to be a Niebuhrian irony in Katz's statement. Was it possible that the establishment of the state of Israel might have made Jews more powerless than they were before?

Jonathan Sarna then chimed in that dual loyalty is not a problem in America. In fact, he implied that dual loyalty is as American as apple pie.

"Dual loyalty comes up in American history differently than it comes up in German history—only in times of warfare, when you do indeed question groups that have historically maintained ties with what they consider to be homeland—Germany, for example, or Japan or England. When there is not a period of warfare, these kinds of multiple loyalties within an American context have always been found acceptable. This has been one of the things that has made America different."

Still, warned Katz, the myth of dual loyalty is strong in some parts of American society. And sadly, this myth drags along with it some very unfortunate anti-Semitic language and ideology.

Neuhaus took the dual-loyalty charge and turned it into an admonition—intended for American Jews and American Christians alike.

"It is important to emphasize that there is obviously a Christian parallel on this question of dual loyalty. That is, if Christians took their theology of the church seriously, they would certainly say that the church as a community takes precedence over national bonds or any other. The charge of dual loyalty has never been leveled against American Protestants as it has been against American Roman Catholics because the Protestants have generally had a very weak doctrine of the church. But with regard to the charge of dual loyalty, Rome is Roman Catholicism's Israel.

"Christians and Jews would both say that to be a good American does not mean that our primary loyalty is to the United States of America religiously. America may be, as Chesterton said, the only nation with the soul of a church. But, none of us would say theologically that America is our church."

Dual loyalty properly understood, therefore, should be a fact of life in America's Jewish and Christian communities. Dual loyalty, Neuhaus suggested, is not a charge to be feared, but a conviction and a reality to be maintained.

Realignment in Progress

Neuhaus framed the last topic of the morning.

"In the early part of this century Jews who thought about such things thought their friends were liberal Christians and, most specifically, liberal Protestants. That is still deeply entrenched institutionally. If it is now true that the pervasive worldview of left-of-center Christianity— Roman Catholic and non-Roman Catholic—has no positive place for Jews, if it is now true that there is no positive understanding of the world-historical role of Judaism or of the moral stature of Judaism, then Jews who think about such things now, it seems to me, must ask themselves what are the implications of this."

Thinking of the average mainline Protestant local church on Main Street, Ronald Sobel guessed that the average member in the average pew had never considered "the world-historical role of Judaism," let alone considered it positively. Most mainline members, he speculated, are indifferent to such questions. Indeed, "they are probably more concerned about the AA group meeting in the fellowship hall on Friday nights," thought Himmelfarb. Undaunted, Neuhaus pressed the question: Is the mainline membership's indifference to the world-historical place of Judaism "filled with peril" for the Jewish community?

Yes it is, answered Lucy Dawidowicz. And the possibility of peril is increased if one looks at recent changes at the leadership levels of the churches.

"There have been very important changes in the churches in the last ten or fifteen years. In the liberal Protestant denominations there has been a move to the left, an intrusion of liberation theology, a preeminence of the Third World outlook, all of which have a fundamental impact on attitudes toward Jews and toward Israel."

Marvin Wilson then emphasized that mainline liberation theology is not so liberating for the Jew and Israel.

"There has been the assumption in mainstream or liberal Protestant circles that the Arab is the underdog, and that the notion of liberation theology does not apply to the Jew or to those in Israel. There has been an overemphasis on the poor, impoverished, and oppressed being in the Arab world, and in the process the Jew has been left out."

American Roman Catholics—not all of them, but some important ones—have also drifted leftward, Himmelfarb noted.

"There has been a remarkable change in Roman Catholicism over the past generation. The last really big encounter that Jews as Jews had with the Roman Catholic Church was the Dreyfus affair in France. There the Catholic Church was against the French Revolution, against the beneficiaries of the French Revolution—namely, the Jews—and against those considered the agents of the French Revolution—Jews, Huguenots, and Freemasons. There were all kinds of lovely things being said. Remember, Jews were the worms gnawing underground at the roots of Christian civilization. Jews knew then what to make of it; the Catholic Church was the enemy. When I was a boy, as I've said, I oriented myself on Cardinal Spellman: if he said something was good, I knew it was bad, and vice versa.

"Now everything has changed. In the old days the Catholic Church was on the right. Now the Catholic Church, or many eminent Catholics, or so many loyal Catholics, are way out on the left. Maryknoll sisters, nuns, are cheering for Marxist-Leninists in Nicaragua. Nuns!

"I'm an old-fashioned Jew, and kind of paranoid and self-centered and myopic, with tunnel vision. But one thing has not changed. Whether Catholics are on the right, as in the time of Dreyfus, or on the left, as now, the Jews get it in the neck. Israel specifically gets it in the neck. Moreover, a regime of liberal democracy, which I think goes hand in hand with capitalism, a regime under which Jews prosper and the only regime under which, I think, Jews can flourish, is the regime that is the specific enemy of this new-leftism in the Catholic Church. Though they do not single out Jews as Jews, they do single out Israel as an enemy and the bourgeois system as well. So de facto, then, the new Catholics are as much, or almost as much, or in intention as much, or in consequence as much against the Jews as the old Catholics were, though there has been a 180-degree change in political orientation—from a reaction and total repudiation of the French Revolution to an embrace of the Russian Revolution. But still the Jews get it in the neck."

As mainline Protestant and Roman Catholic leadership is moving toward the political and ideological left, fundamentalist and evangelical leadership is not. Dawidowicz reminded the conference of the pro-Jewish convictions that the fundamentalist/evangelical community holds.

"Fundamentalists/evangelicals who have come into prominence

in the last ten years have two things going for the Jews. First, they are pro-American. They are not anti-American. They are for this country and what it stands for. Second, they are pro-Israel, whatever the end-time problems are. Sadly, most American Jews are unable to come to terms with this. They see the left as the friend and the right as the enemy."

Pointing to the experiences of the Jewish community with conservatism and liberalism in modern nations, Steven Katz explained to the group that it was easy to understand why the community clings to a friendship with the left.

"The Jewish community historically in the modern world—since the French Revolution and the rise of modern conservative movements in Europe and America—has suffered grievously at the hands of conservative movements, even in democratic, liberal, republican societies. Therefore, in the Jewish community there is a residual antipathy, or fear, of conservative movements that is deep-rooted. Conversely, there is the view that the Jewish community has always fared well in liberal or centrist democratic societies, as represented by the kind of John Kennedy liberal tradition or the F.D.R. tradition. That historical memory, which is very important to the identity of a group, is the strongest factor in the Jewish community regarding political alliances and the like."

It is not quite that easy, objected Himmelfarb. He granted that there is in the American Jewish community and in the heart of the individual Jew a liberal side. But also, he declared, there is in the Jewish community and in the individual Jew a pragmatic—or more conservative—side. Himmelfarb spoke about the conflict between liberalism and pragmatism.

"There is a conflict between the two Jews within the breast of each American Jew. The one is liberal, educated, civic, forward-looking, progressive, and a devoted reader of the *New York Times*. The other always asks, 'Is it good for the Jews? Are they out to get me?'

"Personal anecdote. Twenty years ago I moved into my present house. It is in what they call a 'mixed neighborhood' in White Plains, New York. We were greeted by a Mayflower family that belonged to the local Congregational Church and that was extraordinarily civic. They were delighted that we had moved in. Though we were not quite as good as a black family, we were not Italian. In Westchester County, of course, Italians are the dominant white presence. As a Jew, I could be expected to be civic, forward-looking, progressive, right on the question of public schools, anti–parochial schools, and generally right on all the issues.

"The Congregational Church, which is now the United Church of Christ, is an important participant in the National Council of Churches. And the National Council is, if anything, only a pale reflection of the World Council of Churches. And the World Council is anti-West primarily, and, as a corollary of its being anti-West, it also is anti-Israel.

"I am convinced that the interest of Jews lies in the West—not the South or East. The interest of Jews is in liberal democracy, in the system that prevails in the United States, where there is a distinction between political power and economic power and pluralism, rather than a conjunction of powers as in a socialist regime. For Israel and for Jews, that is their interest.

"There is this contraction and tension within Jews—between the universalist, progressive American on the one hand and the particularistic Jew on the other. To the degree that this becomes pronounced, to the degree that Jews give primacy to the second over the first, there will be realignment."

Rabbi Sobel decided to state that he, for one, gives primacy to the second—that is, Jewish self-interest over Jewish progressivism. Sobel began with a few words on capitalism and implied that the Jewish community must realign.

"Up to this time in the conference the word *capitalism* has not been used once. Capitalism has provided more freedom for more people than any other historic phenomenon that I can think of. That has significant implications for the well-being of the Jewish world. We have flourished under capitalism as we have flourished under no other economic system. All of the political institutions and the cultural manifestations are largely rooted and grounded in that concrete human reality. That is why the leadership of the left-of-center Christendom today is for us anathema and frightening."

Charles Silberman suggested that a Jewish realignment is actually underway.

"I think a degree of realignment is in process. This conference is one piece of evidence of that. The disparity between the views of the Jewish leaders in 1981 and the rank and file is another. The overwhelming number of Jews does not know what the National Council of Churches is, let alone what positions it maintains. So, to the extent that they respond to these questions, their responses are based on memories of organizations having been pro–civil rights or pro-whatever in the past. It takes a fair amount of time to gain some sense about what the National Council and the World Council represent."

But a major obstacle to the Jewish-Christian realignment remains, cautioned Silberman: the Christological language of the Christian right.

"The visceral fears that Jews have, though exaggerated and mistaken in some instances, are not completely groundless. How quickly the realignment will occur will depend in large measure on the speed with which the political leaders of the Christian right can find a new language with which to express their positions. It must be less threatening and not raise so many visceral fears."

Neuhaus tried out this realignment summary on the conference.

"The logic of some kind of realignment seems self-evident to most here. But here we are not simply talking about political alignment. I was a little worried that earlier we were getting excessively political. It seems to me that the much more important realignment involves what we believe—about the West, about democracy, about capitalism. And regardless of the parties and categories involved—left, right, and center (and those alignments are always shifting)—it is on those things that Jews and Christians, if we are going to be talking about the revitalization of the American experiment, have to come together. We have to come together around those ideas, primarily."

Several in the group accepted the opinion that an important realignment is occurring in the realm of culture and ideas. Some, however, did not. Steven Katz, for example. Relying on survey research on Jewish college students for evidence, Katz reported that the group is committed to a liberal—very liberal—set of cultural ideas.

"Take moral-cultural ideas on abortion, premarital sex, drugs, divorce, and all the human elements in interpersonal relations. Fairly recent surveys of college students on these issues show the Jewish group, not surprisingly, to be the most liberal by far. I cannot see a major cultural realignment with regard to those personal ethics."

Milton Himmelfarb responded.

"You move very quickly from cultural outlook to behavior. First, cultural outlook is not necessarily the same as behavior. Second, we at the American Jewish Committee have done Jewish freshmen studies over the years. The Jewish freshmen's cultural attitudes in 1983 were far more conservative than they had been in 1969 and 1971. As a matter of fact, adults who made up the classes of '69 and '71 were less left than they had been in '69 and '71, but more left than their contemporary kid brothers and sisters who were freshmen. The gap between conservative and liberal Jews and socio-economically comparable non-Jews shrank."

Yes indeed, posited Himmelfarb, a cultural realignment is underway.

The meaning of realignment in society is really quite simple: a particular group discovers that other groups that were once friendly are not so friendly now, and that yet other groups that it once considered adversaries can now be considered friends. This, most agreed, is currently happening to the Jewish community in American society. As this realignment progresses, one might ask, what exactly might the Jewish community offer its new allies and the greater society? Rabbi Novak prepared a paper and some comments to respond to that question.

THE JEWISH MISSION IN AMERICA

Rabbi Novak expressed a very firm conviction that the Jewish community has a public responsibility—indeed, a mission—in America. This mission, according to Novak, does not simply involve individual Jews doing their own Jewish thing in public. Instead, it is a mission of the Jewish community as the Jewish community to the larger society. Furthermore, led by Novak, the conferees took up such topics as the sorts of dangers and temptations that might easily distort the Jewish mission, the mission's effort to contribute to the development of a mediating language and a public philosophy, the notion that the mission might learn from the person and work of Reinhold Niebuhr, and the mission's near and distant future.

Pitfalls Everywhere

What Rabbi Novak was proposing in essence was a new model for the Jewish community's participation in American public life. He did not suggest that this model had to be something completely new; to the contrary, he took the "mission of Israel" model, which originated in nineteenth-century Reform Judaism, as his starting point.

Any new, or revisited, mission of Israel in America must beware of the many traps awaiting the effort, traps of the sort that were fatal to the first attempt. One contemporary trap is political, said Novak; some are inclined to make support for Israel their overriding, if not exclusive, concern.

"I remember a number of years ago when I was in Norfolk, Virginia, there was an effort to mobilize support for Israel. The leaders of the Jewish community had a meeting with the rabbis, and they wanted to approach a certain segment of the fundamentalist Christian community that was openly engaged in proselytizing Jews. They could not seem to understand that even though these people were pro-Israel we basically said that we cannot have a common agenda with them. We cannot have a common agenda with people who are openly interested in proselytizing Jews. Granted, a Christian might hope that ultimately everybody becomes Christian, but direct radio and television appeals to Jews only and distortions of Judaism are another matter. We rabbis refused to participate in the common agenda. The others could not understand that. That is the shallowness of the political Jew. He does not even have a cultural apppreciation that the be-all and end-all is not simply political support for Israel, that there are other aspects of Jewish identity involved."

Politics is a part, an important part, of the mission, but politics is not at the heart of the mission, Novak cautioned. He also counseled that the new Jewish mission cannot expect Jewish theology to be authoritative for all of society. This should not be an especially surprising principle for Jews.

"Jews do not derive from theological statements immediately normative ethical statements. But if somebody wants to know what is underlying the entire system and what values are informing it, or if halakhah is ambivalent (and thank God that many times it is ambivalent—I have to make a choice between one approach and another approach), then Judaism incorporates theology to inform the process of judgment and choice.

"In Jewish ethical discourse, there is a certain secularism in the sense that we deal with moral problems in terms of the moral dilemmas that they present. However, we regard our moral discourse as undergirded by theology, and also in key points of decision and of judgment we can invoke theology as a criterion of judgment, subjective judgment, but not as a criterion of the law itself."

Limited theological authority in the agora has definite connections to the church-state issue, said Novak.

"That is exactly the debate that is going on in America today. In other words, when we say that there is separation of church and state, we are correct in that no religious speaker or religious body can say, 'Based upon our theology, this is what Americans must do.' The last example of that (and the results are horrendous—we are still suffering the effects of it in our society today) was national Prohibition. There a certain type of Protestant mentality decided that its theology had something to dictate to the body politic.

"However, the separation of church and state does not exclude religious considerations from being regarded as a general undergirding of the entire system, or religious factors being openly stated in terms of a criterion for subjective judgment. For example, I am opposed to abortion, elective abortion, first because persons have traditionally been protected in our legal system and second because of the whole concept of personhood I see coming out of the Hebrew Bible—the notion of man being created in the image of God and all that that entails.

"Within Judaism itself there is a model of the separation of the sacred and the profane, which is not an absolute separation but a specific separation with a general relation between the two."

Novak's basic contention on theological authority in society was reinforced during the later discussion of mediating language.

Neuhaus had been nodding in agreement, at least for the most part, while Novak held forth. But he had a problem with Novak's view of Prohibition.

"Prohibition was not a case of people saying, 'Thus saith the Lord.' Prohibition was a movement led by the most progressive, enlightened, educated, concerned-for-the-poor, and, not so incidentally, feminist people in society. And then when it turned sour, everybody wanted to blame it on the fundamentalists. In fact, and this is my second point, it actually worked in many ways. It dramatically reduced and in most of the country practically eliminated the use of alcoholic beverages, even though, for a lot of other reasons, it was not good law."

Returning to the mainstream of the discussion, Neuhaus located another of the dangers of the new Mission of Israel in America—accommodationist or sold-out religion. He admitted that he sees a lot of that around.

"We see today an awful lot of religion that wants to be of service to saving Western Civilization or saving America. This comes from different political orientations."

Are we, as Jews and Christians, he wondered, going to fall into the same idolatrous rut by simply undertaking this mission in society, or can we undertake this mission and at the same time manage to avoid the rut?

"Are we—Jews and Christians—confident that, as David Novak suggests, if one is faithfully Jewish/Christian and that that is the reason one is being faithfully Jewish/Christian, that by a felicitous convergence or coincidence it will also be very good for a democratic, pluralistic, liberal society? If one cannot with confidence answer that question affirmatively, then is not one always in danger of letting religion be used for some purpose other than the high purpose of religion, which is to glorify God?

"If we Jews/Christians were really the kinds of Jews/Christians that we ought to be, then we would discover, by felicitous coincidence, that this is also very good for America. If one is not confident about that, the question will always be: Is this a kind of accommodationism in which religion is being employed?"

The way of avoiding the accommodationist rut is also the way of ultimate trust, ultimately trusting in the communitarian work of God.

"The *civitas*, the community that Christians and Jews are most concerned about, is not the political community as such. There is another community—whether it be expressed as Augustine's city of God or whatever. And this assumes a clear recognition, candid and upfront, of the limits of the political. Without that, it would be compromising not to insist that the 'law of God' be implemented in the public arena."

Jonathan Sarna followed with an unusual observation—that the erosion of religious doctrine, belief, and devotion is the product of missionary activity.

"Now, the question is why the idea of the Mission of Israel declined. I think it declined because of the way one becomes a missionary. What happens is that one begins to shape one's mission in such a way that one will attract a very large audience. That's what all missionaries did and do. Why does the group call itself "Jews for Jesus"? They are doing that in order to shape their mission, in order to curry favor, to get maximum adherence. Of course, once Reform Jews did that, then pretty soon, before they knew it, they had reduced Judaism to social action. You therefore have a reaction, and the reaction said (and it was a reaction in part from Orthodox and Conservative Jews), 'Leave all of that aside. Let us strengthen Judaism from within.' And so there was a very great turn inward and away from the public schools and toward a reinvigoration of Judaism."

Sarna preferred the reaction to the mission over the mission itself.

"At that point there ceases to be a mission of Judaism, and instead there is Judaism setting an example. People can knock on the door of the Jewish community and say 'Teach us.' But that is very different from the Mission of Israel. The Mission of Israel involves going out to the Gentiles and preaching. That is very different from the trend that developed, which is that Jews invigorate the tradition, they study the tradition, they learn what can be learned from it, they display by example what they learn from that great library of Judaism. People who look to them may learn from that example. But that is the only way they learn from it.

"We do not want to make what I think is a fundamental Christian error of trying to shape our message in such a way that we will gain adherents. That cheapens the message and leads to the kind of reductionism that we have learned to oppose."

Himmelfarb was puzzled by Sarna's point. After all, he noted, Dean Kelley at the National Council of Churches sees the missionary-intensive Protestant churches of today among the most doctrinally and morally disciplined churches. There is no trade-off, assured Himmelfarb, between the internal strength of a religious community and its external outreach.

Rabbi Novak was stunned by Sarna's somewhat sectarian model of Judaism in (or outside of) public life. He introduced his intervention with a brief analysis of the conference.

"Here we have a situation of a group, primarily of Jews, sitting at this table at this important location in the Jewish community. This group, let us be self-congratulatory, is rather well known in the community and with rather impressive accomplishments. We are brought together by a Lutheran theologian who is very much a social theorist and who wears a clerical collar and who is saying to us, with an evangelical scholar, 'We want to hear what the Torah has to teach.' If that is our situation, what is our attitude? Do we say to Richard John Neuhaus and Marvin Wilson, 'Just look and see what we are doing. We cannot tell you anything. But if you observe us closely, you will learn an awful lot of nice things about how to conduct your society.' They are saying, 'You have something to say to us. Will you please state it to us?'"

Then Novak urged that his own community should respond, for very Jewish reasons, to the Christian inquiry. First, the biblical reason.

"Our tradition, going to the Bible, is that the God who chose Israel is also the God who created heaven and earth. The God who the rabbis saw as so concerned about the pure and impure is also the God who was judging the Roman nation. That is very much indigenous to Judaism.

Now Moshe Feinstein is to be taken seriously, because no matter how uncomfortable he was with the question, he was saying, 'Yes, you do have to respond. And not to respond is a defamation of the Torah.' "

The second reason, deriving from Judaism's traditional style, followed.

"You cannot not have an opinion in Judaism. Judaism has an opinion on anything that is of importance in the world. That is the whole notion of the Torah. It is not just something in the Temple; it is also something that is in the marketplace, it is in the political arena, it is wherever human beings are. And Jews are wherever human beings are. Therefore, you see, we do indeed have something to say."

Novak suggested not only *that* the Jewish community has something to say in public life but also *what* the community has to say there. Novak implied that his community should express both a Yes and a No.

"It behooves people like us to argue that Judaism does not give its endorsement to any political system wholesale, nor should it. And that is where the distinction between the city of God and the city of Man is crucial. The world is not redeemed. The Messiah, as far as Judaism is concerned, has not yet come. And pseudomessianism is a disease of all religions—Judaism in particular.

"However, Judaism desires a society governed by law. So we can give more endorsement to a society that seems to have an objective legal system where rights are protected, where there is due process of law, where people are not exterminated, where people are not rounded up in the middle of the night, and so on. I'm arguing that that is both good for America and good for the Jews, that we can best survive with all of our particularism in that type of atmosphere."

Neuhaus then came back with several reasons why it is especially crucial that the Jewish community's voice be heard in public life at this juncture in American history.

"It is not only that Jews play such a key role in American intellectual-cultural life; and it is not only because of the generally sad way I think that that role has been exercised over the last fifty years. I really do believe with Rabbi Novak that the (and here I will risk the term) Judeo-Christian tradition—our shared biblical tradition, the notion of law, the notion of providential purpose, and the notion of the human person in relation to divine destiny and vocation—does need to be in an identifiably religious way publicly articulated. We must stop being tongue-tied and embarrassed about saying what it is that we believe, what we do indeed believe about how we ought to order our life together. At least for most of us around this table—if scratched very deep or pressed very hard—the reason we believe this is that we believe it is God's will. We believe that it is the revealed nature, structure, and *telos* of reality. It is not simply that it is good for America, or that America has been good to us, or all of those reasons, which are obviously not ultimate reasons but at best penultimate ones or less. There is a lot substantively to be contributed from the Jewish community that has not been nurtured and encouraged.

"There are two other reasons. One I am a little reluctant to put on the record, but it can be stated nicely. I really do believe, without being paranoid, that in the naked public square Jews most particularly are imperiled. Unless you can find some compelling moral-religious-theological-metaphysical reason why this troublesome community must be reverenced, it will not be reverenced for long. I think that is true.

"Then there is a third reason which has to be stated delicately. I do not want to see the kinds of Christians who are presently feeling their oats in redirecting American life have a monopoly on that. And those of us who are not members of moral majoritarianism and the religious new right badly need religiously informed allies. Judaism, if it can be moved in all of its intellectual and spiritual vitalities in America, can play an enormous role in preventing an unhealthy monopoly by the Jerry Falwells of the world."

The consensus seemed to be that the risks that go with attempting a new mission of Israel in America are great. But the risks that go with not attempting the mission are even greater.

Public/Political Philosophizing

If there is to be a new mission of Israel in America, it must, sooner or later, face two formidable challenges: the construction of a public/political philosophy and the development of a vocabulary or language through which that philosophy might be constituted, communicated, and corrected.

The challenge of a mediating language was taken up first. A very unmediated version of a new mission of American Jews, Neuhaus contended, would go something like this: "The halakhah says this, therefore that answers that societal question, that issue." Neuhaus brought similar unmediated approaches to mind.

"We of course also have an evangelical or fundamentalist version of that: the Bible says such-and-such, and is perfectly clear; therefore, biblical law ought to be the law of the land. You have some who take that very, very seriously in the fundamentalist community. For example, in the fundamentalist community are the so-called 'theonomists'—R. J. Rushdoony in California, and a group down in Tyler, Texas, that publishes an enormous amount of material that really follows through with rigor saying that biblical law should be the law of the land and that the task for Christians is to take the land for Christ, for the rule of Christ. They call themselves 'theonomists.' Theocrats is what they are, but not stupidly so. There is some precedent for this in the Puritan tradition."

Opposed to the unmediating way is the mediating way, Neuhaus explained.

"I have argued that what we need is some kind of mediating language in which you move from the theological-metaphysical-meta-historical faith statement to the public arena and find a way in which you can share a vocabulary with people who do not share your presuppositions theologically."

Quite naturally, those who oppose mediating have a handy accusation to use on those who favor mediation, Neuhaus noted, but he is not bothered by the charge.

"Of course a lot of people on the Christian right would say that I have basically bought the secularist proposition, and once I have agreed to do that I have agreed to do exactly what I say people should not do—namely, to check their beliefs at the cloakroom before entering the public arena. I think they are wrong, and I do think there is value in a mediating language."

Next, for the sake of argument or perhaps out of conviction, the conference participants assumed with Neuhaus that a mediating language and a public philosophy are societal goods. Then they were primed to discuss whether or not Jewish life and tradition might contain the beginnings of such a language and such a philosophy.

Milton Himmelfarb had no doubt that Judaism has ties to a particular mediating language—the mediating language of law.

"The mediating language goes this way. It is quite clear that classical, almost unanimous Jewish political theology asserts that there should be a state—be it a democracy, monarchy, or classical republic—governed by law, in which there is neither arbitrary violence nor robbery by the authorities. In the late twentieth century the only empirically valid form of a state ruled by law is liberal democracy. Maimonides did not order liberal democracy; he ordered the rule of law. In the twentieth century the rule of law is, ideally, liberal democracy."

Steven Katz objected to this. He implied that it is not surprising that Judaism does not carry the components of a mediating language. Why? Because Judaism lacks even a primitive political philosophy, upon which a mediating language depends for its very existence.

"The one area of Jewish tradition where we really have no tradition, in the fullest sense of the term, is political philosophy. There is no Jewish political philosophy. There is a prudential philosophy, which says that Jews should stay in their own area and respect the law of the land insofar as it does not force you to break certain fundamental parameters. But we do not have a real political philosophy, as the Catholic tradition has and as the Protestant tradition has. And obviously, that has to do with our lack of political power since the destruction of the Second Temple."

Katz's last sentence caught Neuhaus's attention.

"The suggestion is that first you get power and then you get a philosophy. It is true in the sense that we are saying exactly that about the religious new right. We are saying: 'Here you people of the religious new right are getting power. You sure better get a philosophy pretty soon that is going to reassure us as to how you're going to use this power.'

"In America in this century Jews certainly have had a slice of the power. They certainly have participated and do participate in the power reality of America. If you are right that there is no Jewish political philosophy, it is one reason many Jews in positions of power have sided with the proposition that you can get along without political philosophies. This is another definition of what I mean by the naked public square—it is society trying to live without a political philosophy."

Charles Silberman expressed his agreement with the proposition that there is no political philosophy in Judaism. This is so, he added, because of "the dialectical nature of Judaism. One can find support for almost any position one wants." He then recounted an incident from his public life.

"Ruth Weiss criticized me in *Commentary* for not demonstrating how my liberal-democratic politics grows out of my Judaic values. Had I tried to do so, she would have denounced me for describing inauthentic Judaism. Although I did not try to demonstrate it, I feel deeply in a personal sense that my politics grows out of my understanding of Judaism, which is to say those aspects of the tradition that I seize upon. But I am sufficiently aware that one can equally persuasively argue a conservative view."

Finally, Katz made a statement on the poverty of Judaism with regard to public discussion.

"It is very difficult to look to Jewish tradition, especially to halakhah, to provide the model for a kind of public discourse in American liberal society."

After all, he recalled to reinforce his case, the Jewish communities of history have done some quite illiberal things.

"For example, in eastern Europe there was a whole history where the traditional community opposed emancipation, opposed civil liberties, fought against the Napoleonic reforms, got together regularly to pray that Napoleon would be defeated, was thrilled when he was brought to heel, consistently opposed democratic regimes and democratization and progressive regimes. In Germany, for instance, there were groups that opposed democratic reform."

Marvin Wilson then wondered aloud about the urgency of developing a public philosophy and a mediating language. Jews and Christians share a biblical tradition and broad agreement on social-ethical principles, he reasoned, so why should we be so anxious to build a public philosophy? It seems that our only disagreements arise over how our social-ethical principles are applied in the specifics of policy recommendations.

Neuhaus responded to these assertions.

"It is not the problem that we disagree only when it comes down to the specifics of what ought to be done with regard to the abortion clinic, or what ought to be done about prayer in public schools, and so on. It is said that we can agree on the sacredness of life and respect for dissent and so forth. No we cannot! In our culture we cannot. When Christians and Jews learn to say publicly, in the public arena, the most elementary things, then we will simply say the things that we would all say first—for example, that we are created, that we are creatures, not the creators. This has enormous ramifications, not in the form of answers you come to with regard to genetic engineering and a host of biomedical questions but with the way we discuss and debate and engage one another in arriving at those answers. The answers may be right or wrong, we will make a lot of mistakes, and piety is no guarantee that we will end up with the right answers, but this simple affirmation reshapes the way in which the ethos of a democratic society exercises itself in the always open-ended, always fallible, always mistake-laden process of decision making."

Bowing to Silberman and Katz, Neuhaus acknowledged the difficulty of constructing a political philosophy and an accompanying language from Jewish or other sources. But, he warned, a liberal-democratic society without such societal understanding of the good can easily become a wasteland of warring sects and, worst of all, idolatrous religion.

"I am terribly worried by anybody who thinks that there is a Christian politics, or a Jewish politics, or a biblical politics. Sojourners, an evangelical group, uses that all of the time. They pull a Bible passage and match it with a policy. It is a left fundamentalism. They can do it as much as R. J. Rushdoony on the right. It is abhorrent. Not so much because it is bad politics but because it is blasphemous, because it identifies the absolute with that which is not absolute. It says 'Thus saith the Lord' when the Lord has not said. In other words, it is false prophecy."

Ending this part of the discussion, Neuhaus suggested that the task of public philosophizing might begin with an acknowledgment of something said by theologian Hans von Balthasar. "We got it wrong at the beginning," said Neuhaus, paraphrasing. "It is not *cogito ergo sum*—'I think, therefore I am.' It is *cogitor ergo sum*—'I am thought, therefore I am.'"

Echoing von Balthasar and quoting Bishop Barclay, Milton Himmelfarb contributed a poetic flourish: "We exist because we are in the eye of our creator." Public philosophy, it seems, might best begin in religious affirmation.

Niebuhr's Contribution and Example

It was bound to happen during this conference—a discussion of Reinhold Niebuhr. The biography by Richard Fox (*Reinhold Niebuhr* [New

York: Pantheon, 1986]) had started a greater discussion of the same. Now the conferees were prepared to join in. Himmelfarb primed the group for what was to follow.

"Reinhold Niebuhr was the first among serious American Christian theologians who expressed a respect for and an acceptance of Judaism and Jews, even in their secular capacity and in their irreligious capacity. What does Niebuhr's actual teaching or example have to say to us on these questions?"

Rabbi Novak did not bother to answer Himmelfarb's question, but he did want to commend Neibuhr for his friendship with Abraham Joshua Heschel and for his Protestant brand of political philosophy.

"Most of us would agree that the greatest Jewish theologian in America has been Abraham Joshua Heschel. Heschel said that he could never have launched his career in America and said the things that he said beginning with *Man Is Not Alone* without the daily encouragement of Reinhold Niebuhr.

"Despite the fact that Niebuhr wrote too much, despite the fact that he at times was glib, *The Nature and Destiny of Man* is the most powerful statement of a Protestant political philosophy, which is genuinely Protestant, of any theologian in our time. Look at the social theory, for example, of Karl Barth. Barth's social theory was no different than a nineteenth-century theory. Basically, his argument against Hitler was 'You're encroaching on the church.' He was a very brave man and a wonderful person. But, as Niebuhr pointed out, he had no social philosophy at all; that was a great debate in 1948 in Amsterdam at the World Council of Churches. Paul Tillich started as a religious socialist in Germany, but his career in America was almost exclusively metaphysical-philosophical theology. *The Nature and Destiny of Man*, if you forgot everything else that Reinhold Niebuhr wrote, is a major statement of Protestant Christian political thought that is not relativistic, that is not a situation ethics, that is rooted in the Christian tradition. It is a classic that will endure."

Neuhaus's curiosity was aroused by Novak's comment. "Substantively," he asked, "could the argument of *The Nature and the Destiny of Man* have been made from Jewish sources?"

"Yes," replied Novak, "a large part, if not all, of Niebuhr's major political thought is not deduced from Christology. Christians might have a problem with that. Jews do not."

"Non-Barthian Christians," Neuhaus noted, "also do not have a problem with that."

Lest the group slide into an uncritical opinion of Niebuhr and his political-philosophical work, Neuhaus cautioned that Niebuhr might have been seduced more than a little by the naked public square. Neuhaus drew from John Cuddihy's work.

"Jack Cuddihy has done a very formative piece on Niebuhr in his book *No Offense,* where he deals with Niebuhr, John Courtney Murray, and Arthur Hertzberg. One of Cuddihy's points is that Niebuhr represented precisely the kind of person who trimmed his sails and sublimated particularities in order to fit into the bland mix of a banal kind of notion of what it meant to be an American—in other words, into WASP sensibilities. There is enough in Niebuhr to justify Cuddihy's rather brutal depiction.

"For example, on the question of the Jews, while Abraham Joshua Heschel was grateful for what Niebuhr did in terms of Jewish-Christian relations and specifically on the question of not proselytizing the Jews, Heschel realized the weakness in that. He saw that Niebuhr himself was so safely immune from all of the religious-metaphysical-theological passions that might lead one to missionary activity that it was not really as though Niebuhr was giving anything up. In other words, he was simply cautioning Christians who still had a passion to preach Christ that they ought not preach Christ at Jews. That reduced somewhat the credibility or the impact of Niebuhr's breakthrough statements with regard to Jewish-Christian relations."

It was suggested that, as the title from an article that Michael Novak wrote for *Commentary* in the early 1970s has it, American society certainly does "need Niebuhr again." But it seemed clear to a couple of conferees that more than Niebuhr is needed today.

The Jewish-Christian Future in America

What Reinhold Niebuhr lacked in the public square—a definite, unashamed hold on and identification with religious particularities—is an absolutely essential element of the Jewish-Christian future in America, if that future is to be all that it can be. Jews and Christians being nice to each other (by gathering for tea-and-sympathy sessions) is all well and good, but that will not sustain the public task of the synagogue and the church. Polite conversation is to be welcomed, but neither will that sustain the public vocation of Judaism and Christianity in America. What is needed, Rabbi Novak urged, is devout Jews and devout Christians preserving their particularities yet consensually collaborating for their public duty.

"If people with important backgrounds and positions, who are deeply committed to their traditions—not superficial Christians or superficial Jews—can on certain issues consensually say, 'From where we come, this is what we think society should do and this is what we think it should not do,' that will be a very compelling moral type of persuasion, not coercion. Why? Precisely because we are fully recognizing the fact that for most of our history we were at each other's throats and wanted nothing to do with each other.

"This consensus has to be more profound than the old-time good-will consensus. I have argued that if you really want unity, secularism offers the cheapest unity of all. You just drop all the particulars. Yet this proves to be so shallow and hollow that it will not stand up to anything."

Ronald Sobel took a more economic-poetic tack on the question of the future, introducing his statement with a comment on economic change today.

"It has been pointed out that in the Western world (and it is fast happening in the rest of the world), for the first time in human history more people are gainfully employed in the delivery of services than in labor-intensive tasks. The major economic business of the Western world (and it is fast becoming the major economic business of the entire world) is no longer what is dug out of the earth or planted on the earth, but the gathering, the refinement, the organization, and the transmission of knowledge. It is called the knowledge revolution.

"At the same time most of the world's enterprises are no longer confined to nation-states. The multinational corporation, trans-nationalism, and globalism are the order of the day.

"Today we do not have to appropriate nature or exploit human nature. The main business is knowledge. And what is the value of knowledge if it is just held on to? By its very nature, knowledge is diffused. You share it. When the major commodity is knowledge, you are tapping and utilizing not the concrete things of the earth but the abstract laws of nature.

"What we—Jews and Christians—share in common, down deep, is the belief that we are created, that we are not the creators. In keeping with that assumption, if we are utilizing the abstract laws of nature as the source of this knowledge/information, then ultimately we are tapping the mind of God.

"So the world becomes smaller as it becomes larger. No longer limited to time and place, we are really truly conscious of the process of becoming, of the openness of history. Therefore, the new paradigm. If all of this is emerging, then how in the heck do you explain it to the Ayatollah mentalities? The Ayatollah mentalities—whether in Christendom, in Islam, or in Judaism—are threatened by this new emerging world. And they want to stop it. But the best they can do is put a brake on it. This can be very painful, but it will not stop the new world. Now, where are we and what do we do when they cannot stop it?

"What are our possibilities? We can talk to each other. We can share in a way that perhaps has never been open to us in history before. There is a possible fifth force operating in the universe that Galileo did not know about, that Einstein did not know about. Who knows what the possibilities are? What is suggested is that diversity is very much the order of the day. We might just find that at this point in time diversity is God's will."

As John Courtney Murray once claimed, "Pluralism is written into the script of history."

Next, Neuhaus set forth a call to covenant commitment.

"What we need between Jews and Christians in this society is a sense of a shared adventure in covenantal trust and fidelity. We can embark on this journey in trust because we believe that it is enshrouded by and insured by and ultimately consummated in covenantal promise. Christians need to come, for theological reasons, to reverence Jews—not simply tolerate but reverence all humanity, but Judaism and Jews in a most particular way. I think we are far beyond Saint Paul's puzzling and agonizing in Romans 9–11, where he goes through this problem about how it could be that the Messiah's own people did not accept him. I do not mean to sound sacrilegious or to claim that we understand this better than Paul. But we do understand some things better than Paul. A lot has happened that Paul did not know about; in fidelity to Paul, we can reflect upon that in a Pauline manner. One of the things that Christians are coming to understand is that in the script of history there is a relationship of trust and interdependence between Christians and Jews which is absolutely open-ended. This in no way denies the fact that I think that Jesus is the Alpha and the Omega or that in the ultimate epiphany in which we see no longer though a glass darkly but face to face all Jews will recognize Jesus of Nazareth as the Messiah. The only question is whether he has come for the first time or the second time. That is really the critical difference between Christians and Jews.

"To be a Jew and to be faithful to that tradition is a holy obligation. There is no answer, and I cannot imagine that there could be before the kingdom comes, to the paradox of fidelity to Judaism and the call to faith in Christ. Heschel and I went back and forth on this for a long, long time. Heschel really wanted me to say that I did not want him to be a Christian. To which my response was, 'I am not permitted to say that. But neither am I mandated to say that you ought to become a Christian. What you ought to do is follow God's will as God is calling you. It is my concern, as your brother in covenant, to make sure that you do nothing that violates your divine vocation.'

"It is that profoundly, theologically grounded, peculiar relationship between Jews and Christians which can help us together to speak a word of hope to a world which sees that open-endedness as utterly threatening and as promising nothing but chaos. To that we can speak the word of promise, which is essentially the Jewish-Christian word of the covenant."

On that word, the word of covenant, the conference ended. But in that word, it might be said, the Jewish-Christian future commences. And it just might be that in the Jewish-Christian future lies the future also of the experiment known as America.

Participants

Naomi Cohen
Department of History
Hunter College

John Cuddihy
Department of Sociology
Hunter College

Lucy S. Dawidowicz
Author

Ed Dobson
Fundamentalist Journal

Milton Himmelfarb
American Jewish Year Book
Institute of Human Relations

Irving Louis Horowitz
Department of Sociology
Livingston College
Rutgers University

Steven Katz
Department of Near Eastern Studies
Cornell University

William Kluback
Department of Social Sciences
Kingsborough Community College
City University of New York

Richard John Neuhaus
The Rockford Institute
Center on Religion & Society

David Novak
Jewish Theological Seminary of
America

Michael Novak
American Enterprise Institute

Stanley Rothman
Department of Government
Smith College

Jonathan D. Sarna
Center for the Study of the American
Jewish Experience
Hebrew Union College–Jewish
Institute of Religion

Charles Silberman
Author

Howard Singer
H. Daniel Singer Associates, Inc.

Ronald B. Sobel
Temple Emanu-El
New York City

Paul T. Stallsworth
The Rockford Institute
Center on Religion & Society

Marvin R. Wilson
Department of Biblical Studies
Gordon College

118

Index of Names

Abram, Morris B., 6
Adler, Felix, 46, 47
Augustine, Saint, 23, 107
Baeck, Leo, 46
Baal Shem Tov, Israel, 58
Balthasar, Hans von, 113
Barth, Karl, 80
Bellah, Robert, 82
Bennett, William, 6
Bernadin, Joseph, 26, 75
Bonhoeffer, Dietrich, 38
Boschwitz, Rudolph, 6
Buber, Martin, 21
Carter, James Earl, 28
Chrysostom, John, 23
Cohen, Hermann, 46
Cohen, Naomi, 7, 13
Cohen, Steven M., 1, 2
Craven, Avery, 51
Cuddihy, John, 114
Durkheim, Emile, 4
Eisenhower, Dwight D., 11
Eckstein, Yechiel, 35
Einhorn, David, 46
Etchegaray, Roger, 34
Falwell, Jerry, 33, 34, 77
Felsenthal, Bernhard, 16

Feinstein, Moshe, 48-49, 109
Flannery, Edward H., 22, 31, 97
Flusser, David, 33
Franklin, Benjamin, 11
Gladden, Washington, 81
Graham, Billy, 34
Greenwald, Michael, 33
Haberman, Joshua, 27
Handy, Robert T., 9, 13
Henry, Jacob, 12
Hertzberg, Arthur, 37, 115
Heschel, Abraham Joshua, 21, 22, 40, 114, 117
Hirsch, Emil G., 46
Hutchinson, William Thomas, 50, 51
ibn Abi Zimri, David, 53
Ignatius of Antioch, 23
Innocent III (pope), 23
Jefferson, Thomas, 15, 83
John XXIII (pope), 25
Justin Martyr, 23
Kahane, Meir, 37
Kant, Immanuel, 46
Kaplan, Mordecai M., 47
Katz, Jacob, 98
Kelley, Dean, 108
Kennedy, James, 75

119